NATURE W
NORTHA

Brian Webster
and
Ron Wilson

Illustrated by Colin Tidbury

JEMA PUBLICATIONS

Published 1999 by Jema Publications

ISBN: 1-871468-88-4

Publisher's Note

Every care has been taken in the preparation of this book. The publishers cannot accept responsibility for any inaccuracies or for any loss, damage or inconvenience resulting from the use of this book.

Jema Publications
40 Ashley Lane
Moulton
Northampton
NN3 7TJ

Jacket Design, Layout, Repro and Printing
by The Design MAP ☎ 01604 231236

CONTENTS

Acknowledgements iv

By Way of Introduction 5

Northampton - Map of the Walks 8

The Walks:

1. Abington Park 9
2. Bradlaugh Fields 13
3. Dallington Heath 18
4. Delapre Park 20
5. Eastfield Park 24
6. Thornton's Park 28
7. Kingsthorpe Mill Local Nature Reserve 30
8. Lings Wood Local Nature Reserve 34

The River Nene Walks:

9. Upton to Duston Mill Meadow 40
10. Duston Mill Meadow Nature Reserve 42
11. South Bridge to West Bridge 44
12. Cow Meadow to Weston Favell Mill 46

Around the Town Centre 51

Looking at Walls 56

Pocket Parks 72

Playing Your Part 76

Your Garden Nature Reserve 85

How Can I Help? 92

Index 95

ACKOWLEDGEMENTS

A number of people have provided information for the book. In particular we would like to thank Chris Gerrard of the Wildlife Trust for Northamptonshire for information on the nature reserves which the Trust manages. Sue Paice, Pocket Parks Officer has, as always been most helpful and supplied information and advice on the Pocket Parks. Peter Nalder of South Court Environmental supplied material, and Colin Tidbury produced the delightful illustrations. Finally, our thanks to Tony Noble of Jema Publications, for his patience and encouragement.

MAPS

These have been simplified for clarity to show the main roads, walks and parks and do not include many of the minor roads.

All the maps are based upon the Ordnance Survey Maps and reproduced with permission of The Controller of Her Majesty's Stationery Office,

BY WAY OF INTRODUCTION

I stand overlooking a sweep of grassland. It is summer, the afternoon sun beating out of a clear blue sky, with just enough breeze to make it pleasantly hot, but not unbearably so. The tall grasses are enlivened with flowers, amongst them the feathery-leaved yarrow with massed blossoms spread like white tablecloths to attract insect visitors. A male meadow brown, our commonest butterfly, was feeding on one of them, its underwings surprisingly orange for a supposedly dull creature. Bees and hoverflies commute from flower to flower, the former with pollen baskets stuffed to overflowing. An animated darning needle of the brightest powder-blue and black turns out to be a damselfly, a refugee from the river a couple of hundred metres away.

Ragwort is here too, its yellow stars a magnet to insects. The deeply-cut leaves, which give it its name, are food for caterpillars, coloured black and orange-yellow in vertical hoops. They have reduced the leaves almost to skeletons. These are the larvae of the cinnabar moth. The adults are equally gaudy with wings of crimson and charcoal-grey. Their colours are nature's way of warning that they are definitely not good to eat.

A few metres away are several wind-sown buddleia bushes - the butterfly bush - with spires of lavender-coloured flowers just beginning to open. Already their heady scent is proving irresistible to butterflies and bees. Several small tortoiseshells jostle with orange- and buff-tailed bumblebees.

A couple of ragged peacocks, one with the tip of a wing gone, a scar from a lucky escape from a small bird on the lookout for a meal also feed. An exotic recent arrival from Mediterranean shores flashes its salmon-pink wings before settling on the topmost spray of buddleia flowers, to reveal itself as a painted lady. A red admiral - red admirable to the eighteenth-century butterfly-hunters who first gave it a name - opens its wings to show velvety-black, scarlet, and pure white, with a hint of blue. Next to the butterfly-bush, over-topping it by more than 60 cms, is a Far East alien, introduced a century or so ago to grace larger gardens. The seeds, borne on the wind, established it as an escapee, and it is now a weed of neglected ground, hedgerows and woodland. This is Japanese knotweed, an aggressive grower, which has shouldered aside its competitors. In winter it dies back to a bundle of sticks which rattle in the cold winds. Towards the end of March the red shoots of new growth appear, almost shyly at first, then seemingly racing one another to reach the sunlight, eventually becoming four metres in height, with huge roughly halberd-shaped leaves. These are followed in August by bunches of white flowers like tiny grapes. Stealthily its underground roots - rhizomes - annually filch more territory for itself, and left alone it quickly dominates an area.

Here too are several shrubby cotoneasters, not planted by humans but by birds which have dropped the seeds as they sat on the fence. They add their own harvest of berries in autumn, and their evergreen leaves are welcome shelter on a winters' night to flocks of house sparrows, which gather there in noisy array before flying to their roost in nearby ivy.

Japanese Knotweed

This area, so rich in wildlife, is not on the very edge of town as you might think, but in the centre. The grassy sward measures a mere five metres each way in a triangle where Silver Street and King Street intersect. Opposite in one direction is the 'Newt and Cucumber,' a pub known to older residents as the 'Criterion.' In front is the Moat House, while behind you is Northampton's Fish Market. We did not set out to deceive, but merely to show you that wildlife interest is to be found wherever you look. In this book we will cover many of the spots within town where you may seek and observe wildlife.

In the following pages you will be able to take many nature walks in Northampton, and discover what a wealth of wildlife there is right on your own doorstep. During the walks, we point out some of the more interesting features. But nature is constantly changing, and what may be seen one month, may not be there the next. Whenever you decide to take a 'nature walk' you will discover so much which will open your eyes to the wonders of the natural world.

THE WALKS

These are numbered to correspond to the Content list

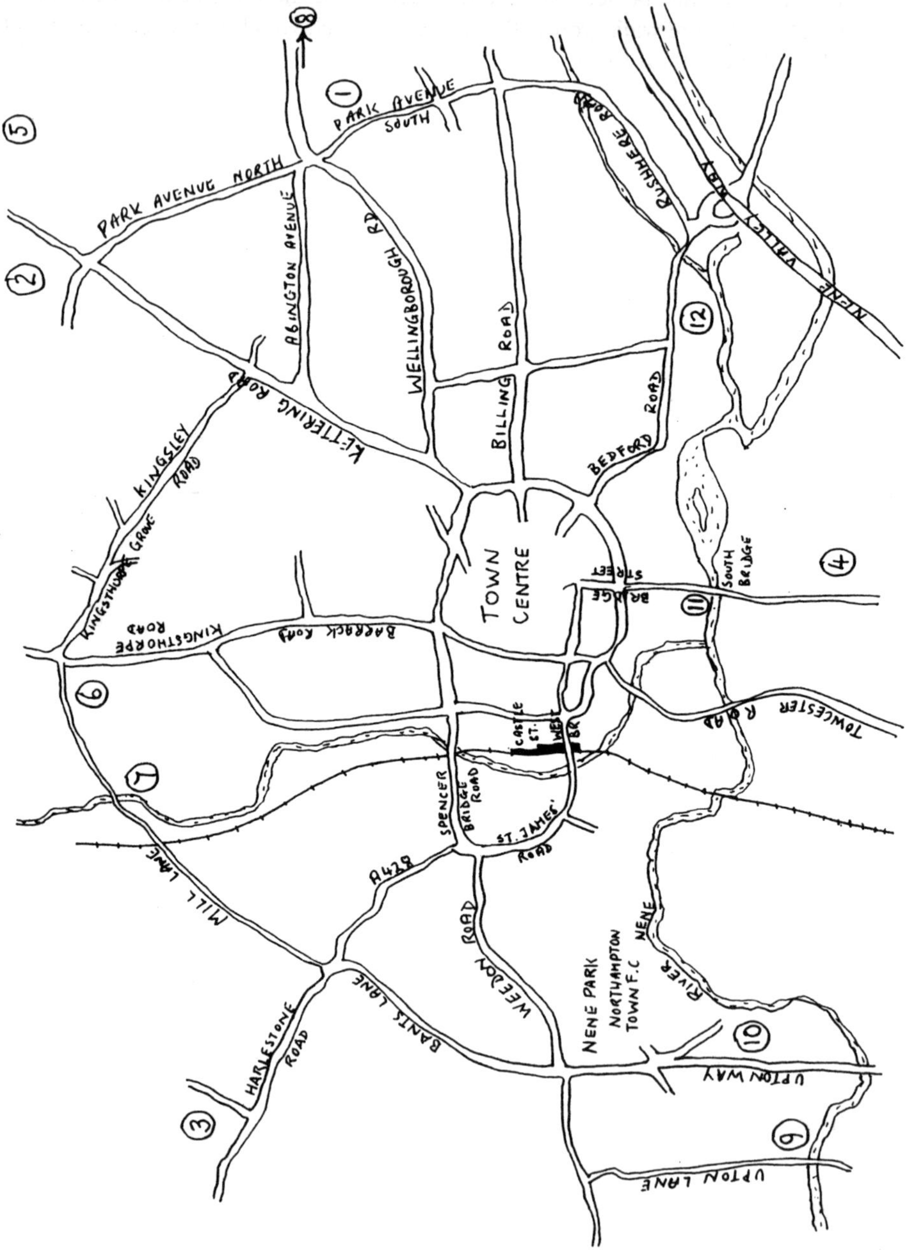

ABINGTON PARK

Find the Park 3km to the east of the town centre, along the Wellingborough Road. Turn right when you get to the Abington public house. Parking is on nearby streets.

In 1893 when the Lady Wantage offered the manor house and part of the park as a gift to the town, it was eagerly accepted by the town elders. Even at this time the Victorian redbrick expansion of Northampton was threatening to engulf it, and so by opening up the park to the townsfolk they were provided with a much-needed green lung: a place in which to escape from everyday cares, a function which it still fulfils today.

Although there have been some wildlife losses over the past years, the park has much of interest. Partly as a legacy of its earlier days, and partly due to the foresight of the town council, its trees are a major feature, with rare species aplenty. Many of them are labelled to make life easier for both tree enthusiast and lay person. Only a few are mentioned here; a full day would be needed to seek them all out.

At the side of the manor house which faces the road, and where the church is to your right, there is a lawn in front of you which is surrounded by a low iron fence. Here there are two mulberry trees. Lady Elizabeth Barnard, who was Shakespeare's favourite grand-daughter, lived at the manor, and is buried at the church. When the great Shakespearean actor David Garrick stayed here he planted the first tree, which was taken as a cutting from the Bard's garden at Stratford. A plaque reads, *'This tree was planted by David Garrick, Esq., at the request of Ann Thursby, as a growing testimony of their friendship, 1778'.*

Mulberry comes from Asia, but is grown in Britain either for its fruit, or as an ornamental tree. Hidden by the heart-shaped leaves, the fruits look like raspberries. Green at first, they gradually turn yellow, then orange, and red, and finally almost black. When over-ripe they have a fine sharp taste, and are very juicy and mouth-watering. The best mulberries are not picked off the tree, but from the ground beneath it, that is if you can beat the blackbirds and thrushes to the feast!

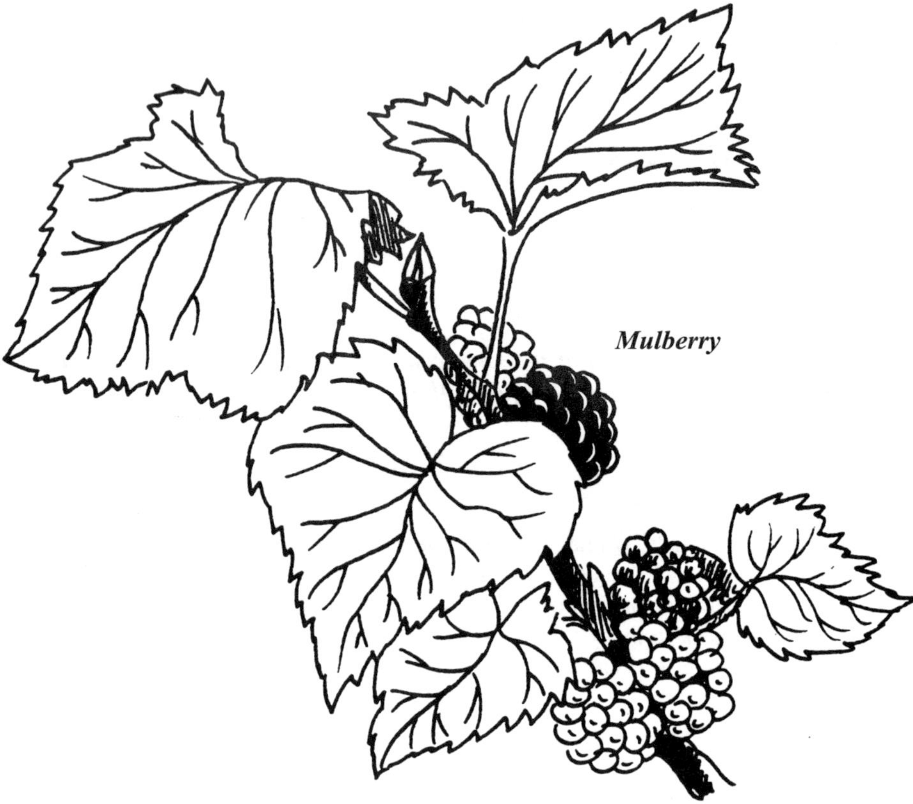

Mulberry

Follow the path around to the other side of the manor, keeping the house on your left, and you come to the aviaries, which are full of colourful birds. Halfway along on the right are two magnificent conifers, a Wellingtonia and a Chile pine. The Wellingtonia was named by the botanist John Lindley, after the first Duke of Wellington. As a wild tree it is rare, found only in the Sierra Nevada of California, where it can grow to over 100 metres tall, measures 27 metres around its trunk, and weighs 1,500 tons. Some Wellingtonia's are over 4,000 years old. So this one is a mere sapling! The bark may be over 30 cms thick, and is soft and spongy. You may punch it hard without hurting yourself. It is sometimes called the 'punch tree' for this reason. For such a large tree it has tiny needles, and the cones are only about 8 cms long.

To you and I the Chile pine may be better known as the monkey puzzle tree. Spanish explorers brought it to Europe in the 18th century. In 1795 Archibald Menzies, was served its seeds as part of a banquet while he was in Chile. He saved some seeds and grew five little plants on the voyage home to England. It was Charles Austin who christened it the monkey puzzle, due to its spiny foliage. There was a craze for growing it in Victorian times, and almost every garden, large or small, had one. Many of these languished and became stunted and ugly, but in ideal conditions it makes a spectacular tree.

If you stand by the Manor House - the museum of today - and face away from the entrance there is a path to your left which has the churchyard wall, also on the left. Take this path, fringed with variegated-leaved hollies, and pass the great beech tree at the churchyard gate. The bare ground here is due to the leafy canopy of the trees, which is so thick that it allows little sunlight to reach the earth. In the early spring a brief carpet of shiny green heart-shaped leaves appears, to be followed by the glistening yellow stars of lesser celandine. This plant, found mainly in woodlands and shady places, is able to put forth its flowers and set seed before the leaves on the trees grow dense enough to steal the sunlight from them. By the time the beech has spread its canopy the ground-hugging celandine has died back, and the energy from its short spell of activity stored underground, either in little white root tubers, or in bulbils found tucked between the stem and leaves.

Continue walking up a gentle slope, and about 50 metres further on look out for a Ginkgo or maidenhair tree on the right. In leaf it is unmistakable; its fan-shaped leaves, notched at the tip, are so unlike those of any other living tree. And this is why it is so special, for it is a living fossil. Its relatives can be traced unchanged into the fossil record for more than 350 million years. In imagination we are whisked back to an age when plants were only just beginning to colonise the land; when the first insects and spiders were evolving from sea-living ancestors; and when lumbering amphibians lived along muddy shorelines. Even the dinosaurs were hundreds of millions of years into the future, while the line that led to humankind had not even hauled itself out of the sea.

If you walk along to the road, and cross over it, the path leads down to the largest of the three lakes. Here you will be greeted by a motley crowd of ducks, expecting you to provide a meal of bread. Almost all of them are descended from the mallard or wild duck. No two of them are alike, but despite their range of colours, it is still possible to pick out the males, which have a few curly tail-feathers. Even in the jostling crowd the pairs tend to stick together. Look for the true wild-type mallard among them. In the breeding season it is a handsome bird with shining bottle-green head, a white neck-ring, and chestnut breast. The loud quacking comes from the females; the male has quite a feeble-sounding call by comparison. Among the mallards there is often a moorhen, large-footed yet seeming to make slow progress as it swims, because it lacks webbing between its toes to help it. At first glance it is a dull bird, but if you look more closely you will see that it has various shades of soft grey, with a greenish tinge to the back, green legs, a bright red beak with a yellow tip, and a series of white chevron stripes along its sides. Upset it and it will rush off flirting two oval white patches under its tail, a warning to others that danger threatens. Together with the mallards the moorhens breed on the islets, safer from the disturbance that is inevitable around the shoreline. The related coot, velvety-black with a white beak and patch on the forehead, also lives here. Quarrelsome birds they flog the water as they furiously chase rivals from their territories. On a recent visit to the lake a pair of Canada geese were evidently intending to set up home on one of the islets.

Moorhen

Having strolled around this lake, follow the path as it skirts the woodland, to the lower lake. Here there are two lovely plants worth seeking out. Both introduced, they often escape from our gardens, and so are included in most wild flower books. Both are geraniums, found naturally in the damp mountain woodlands of Italy and southern Europe. When they are in flower, between May and August, they are easily recognised. First is the pencilled cranesbill, up to 80 cms tall, with hairy-leaves, and flowers of white or palest pink, veined with deep violet. On close examination it is stunningly beautiful. Almost as spectacular is the dusky cranesbill, its flowers rich maroon to almost black, with the petals turned back upon themselves.

These are some of the highlights of Abington Park. There are so many others. So, pause awhile and, according to season, listen and watch for birds, and look for other wild flowers.

BRADLAUGH FIELDS

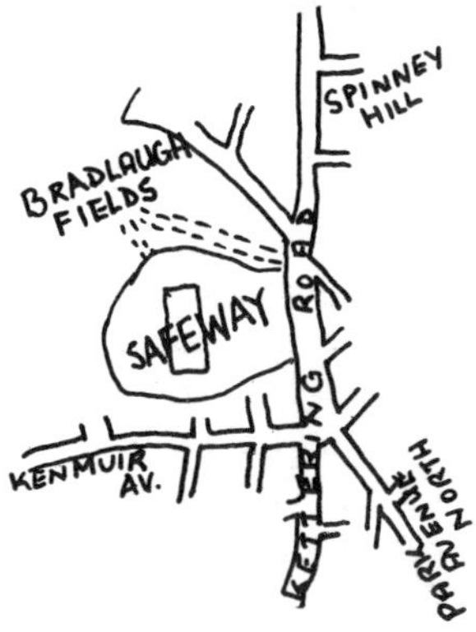

From Northampton centre take the Kettering Road. After 4km look for the Safeway Supermarket on the left.

Bradlaugh Fields, off the Kettering Road, and 'behind' the Safeway Supermarket, is Northampton's newest town park. It was named after Charles Bradlaugh, who was elected MP for Northampton in 1880. A former golf course, this 100 acre site has an abundance of wildlife and as a consequence contains two Local Nature Reserves, which are managed by the Wildlife Trust for Northamptonshire. These two sites, called the Hills and Holes and the Scrub Field, occupy almost 40 per cent of the Park's area.

Compared to Northampton's other parks, which are of traditional Victorian variety with short mown grass for amenity value, Bradlaugh Fields is in stark contrast, with different mowing regimes. Areas of long grass are left to allow plants to flower and set seeds, and these contrast sharply with those which are close mown for ease of access.

The Scrub Field covers 5ha (12 acres) of limestone grassland, where 182 species of plants have been recorded. They include the corn parsley, a slender white-flowered cousin of the more familiar keck or cow parsley of our waysides. Unlike keck,

Knapweed broomrape

however, corn parsley is very rare; rare enough indeed to qualify for inclusion in Northamptonshire's Red Data Book, being found at only two other sites within the county. It flowers quite late in the season, and is best looked for around the middle of August.

Bee orchid

The field also has one of the largest colonies of knapweed broomrape in the county. Knapweed broomrape is one of the 'oddest' of all plants. At its prime towards the middle of June, it appears unhealthy-looking, and pinkish-brown in colour. About a foot or so tall it stands out like a sore thumb amid the greenery of the surrounding vegetation. A close look reveals that it always grows next to a greater knapweed plant, and this is no accident. Knapweed broomrape is a parasite, foisting its own roots onto the root system of its host, and obtaining all of its nutriment from it. True to its name this species is parasitic upon the knapweed, and with such a way-out lifestyle it is perhaps not surprising that it is not very common in Northamptonshire.

Its flowers are not unlike those of the deadnettles and botanists usually place it close to them in their family tree of classification. The tubular two-lipped flowers are eagerly visited by long-tongued bees for the sake of the rich supplies of nectar that they hold. A single flower-spike is capable of ripening 100 000 seeds, each one as fine as dust. With such an output, why is it that our fields are not knee deep in knapweed broomrape plants? This is partly explained by the fact that its host-plant is itself uncommon, and only grows in certain types of undisturbed grassland where the soil has a limey content. The seed, being so tiny, only has sufficient food stored within it to last a day or two after germination. In that short time it has to find the roots of its host, otherwise it will die. Then, once it has germinated, it has to shoulder off the competition from the seedlings of all other species surrounding it. So, despite this vast output of seeds, each broomrape plant needs only one of its seeds to make it to the reproductive stage to guarantee its own survival. Any more and we could in truth be knee deep in knapweed broomrapes.

Restharrow is also found here. Belonging to the pea family, its clear pink flowers are a delight in summer. Its hairy stems, which creep along the ground, have many small pointed oval leaves. It was disliked by the ploughboy of old because its tough, wiry stems and roots would stop his horse-drawn harrow dead in its tracks - it would 'arrest the harrow' - hence the name of restharrow. And when this happened he would be faced with the bother of untangling the plant from his implement.

Both the bee orchid and the relatively common spotted orchid occur on the thin soils of this site. Amongst the most beautiful of all wild flowers, both have 'impossible' lifestyles. The bee orchid grows to about half a metre tall under ideal conditions, but here it usually reaches about 30 cms. Its strikingly beautiful flowers are in shades of pale pink, yellow and deepest red-brown. The pouch-like hairy lip is exaggerated to look like the body of a bumble bee. It also produces chemicals, which mimic the perfume of a female bee. In southern Europe, where it is very common, these flowers prove irresistible to solitary male bees of a certain group. They land to examine what looks like a receptive female bee, and are bowled over the alluring perfume. By the time they discover that they have made an awful blunder it is too late - they have pollinated the flower. Being unable to resist the temptation they move to the next flower and make the same mistake all over again. It seems that in Britain the flowers are mainly pollinated by the wind. The bee orchid sometimes grows in unexpected places. Some years ago I was telephoned with the news that one was in flower in the garden of a staff house at the Princess Marina Hospital in Duston. Disbelievingly, I went to see it, and there it was in all its glory, the plant covered with a little wire cage to protect it.

The spotted orchid is named for the prominent deep purple blotches on its leaves. Its spikes of pink flowers, seen close to, have spots and lines of magenta. These form a pattern of 'guide-lines', which lay out a flight path for visiting bees. Both these species, like most native orchids, depend on an underground association with fungi in order to survive. They have thousands of minute seeds, which may be carried long distances on the wind. Like the broomrapes, they carry only sufficient nutriment for a few days, and in that time must be found by their fungus partner in order to survive. Some orchids take fifteen years from germination to their first flowering. So please admire them but DO NOT PICK THEM. Leave them for others to enjoy. The best time to see them is from mid to late June. Remember, too, that it is an offence to interfere with any protected species, and to uproot any others.

Certainly the most interesting of this group of uncommon plants in The Scrub Field is a dainty little fern, scarcely 5 cm high, called the adder's tongue fern. Last seen at this site in 1983, it was thought to be extinct, probably as a result of the field being bulldozed by the previous owners who wanted to prevent it from becoming a Site of Special Scientific Interest (SSSI) Then in 1997, amid great excitement, a clump of about ten plants was re-discovered. The adders-tongue fern was alive and well, along with all the other fascinating plants of this site, and despite all they had suffered over the previous decade or more.

When you see the plant, you may be tempted to wonder what all the fuss was about. It consists of a single green frond which stands vertically. Arising from its centre is a soft fleshy dark green blade which, with its stem, looks like the tongue of a snake thrusting out, and this is how it came by its name. The herbalists of old used the 'Doctrine of Signatures' by which a plant was supposed to sign its herbal use by its appearance. In 1657 Coles wrote a book called *'Adam in Eden'* in which he states that: " ...out of every leaf it sendeth forth a kind of Pestal like unto an adder's tongue; it cureth the biting of serpents." As late as 1854 Phebe Lankester, in her book *'A Plain and Easy Account of the British Ferns,'* wrote ".. even now large quantities of it are gathered in the villages of Kent, Sussex and Surrey, and prepared according to the old prescriptions."

Other interesting plants include the yellow toadflax, field scabious, and the common fleabane. In the nearby hedgerows there is plenty of ivy and snowberry, which supports a good colony of the dainty little holly blue butterfly. In some years the butterfly is quite common; in others almost non-existent.

After it had been ploughed, the area was not managed, and the main problem now is scrub invasion, hence the reserve's name. The Wildlife Trust has put into operation a management programme of scrub clearance and grass cutting, which will help to eradicate the problem.

The Hills and Holes site is made up of 8ha (20acres) of grassland which, due to its topography, has calcareous grassland on the hill tops and more neutral/slightly acidic grassland in the bottom. Limestone was once quarried on the site, hence the undulating nature of the area.

Both meadow saxifrage, and field mouse ear, which are county rarities, occur in large numbers in the area. Harebells - the bluebell of Scotland - is also present, and flourishes in dry places, It flowers from July to September. The area is surrounded by hedges, some of which date back to at least medieval times. One, known as Holton Lane, is a double hedge and bank.

The area has been saved because of concerted efforts by local people, together with groups like the Wildlife Trust for Northamptonshire. Originally earmarked for housing, it is now available for local people to enjoy. The opinions of local people are constantly sought and monitored on the future of the Park, and this is done through a Management Committee which brings together the Wildlife Trust, the Borough Council, local schools and colleges and the local inhabitants.

Rich in other wildlife, three badger setts occur in the areas, and 20 ha (50 acres) are soon to be added with land from the Commission for New Towns being handed over to the Borough. This will effectively add a further 4.5 ha (11 acres), known as The Quarry Field.

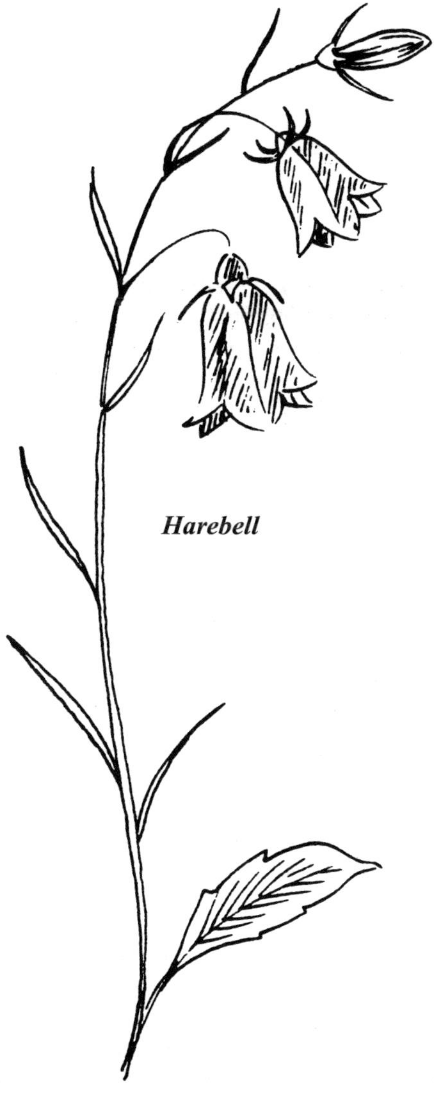

Harebell

DALLINGTON HEATH

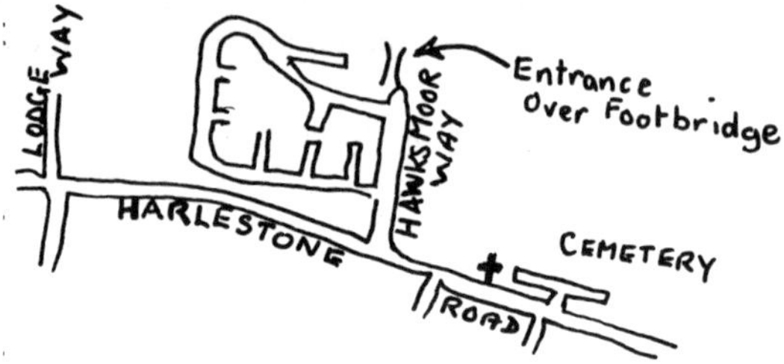

Take the A428 (signposted Rugby) from the town centre, and travel along the Harlestone Road for 6km. Dallington Heath is on the north-western boundary of Northampton, beyond the King's Heath estate. Approach by a footpath through the narrow belt of trees at the bottom of the hill, off Hawksmoor Way, a turn off the Harlestone Road, opposite the Hopping Hill pub.

This is a wildlife area that you would be well advised to visit sooner rather than later, as plans are well advanced to cover this green field site with tarmac, 2 000 houses, industry, and all of the services demanded by such a development - some might say a new town grafted uneasily onto an already top-heavy urban conurbation. At the heart of Dallington Heath are some 32ha (80 acres) of national archaeological importance, which is to be excluded from the main development.

I have known and visited the area for close on half a century, and have watched the unstoppable creep of housing and industry come closer and closer. Where the nationally declining corn bunting was once common, and even quail could be heard calling during the summer, there will soon be bricks and mortar.

A friend and I looked at this site recently to see if it had retained any of its considerable botanical interest. Visiting the site in September is not the best time for such a survey, as many of the annual plants have long since flowered, set seed, and died off. Despite this we discovered, among a total of some 80 species, the cornflower which has not been seen in the wild in our county for half a century. Its vivid blue flowers, smaller than the ones which we cultivate in our gardens, were past their best, but there were still some twenty plants surviving. In all there were five wild flower species which are regarded as uncommon or rare in the county.

Another one-time weed of the farmers' crops is the exquisite corn marigold. Actually a chrysanthemum, its golden flowers sparkle from the grass like miniature suns. Offset by typically grey-green leaves, it is one of the plants which has been virtually eliminated by modern herbicide sprays. Here there were many plants, coming to the end of their flowering period. Ironically, a district on the eastern side of the town, on similar soil to this, actually bears one of the folklore names of this plant - Goldings. Like many of the plants found in cultivated fields, corn marigold relies on disturbance of the soil to expose its long-dormant seeds to start them into growth. In some places the activities of the road-builders have done just that, and for a season or two it brightens up the verges on some of the newer roads such as the A14.

The curiously-named corn spurrey is another uncommon species found here. The name means 'to scatter', and refers to the way the plant scatters its ripe seeds. Somewhat sticky to the touch, it has white flowers in loose clusters, each about a millimetre across, followed by seeds borne on long stalks, which gives the plant quite a bushy and hoary appearance.

Blue fleabane is common here, but described as occasional elsewhere in the county. The word 'fleabane' comes from the fact that the plants of this family were used to discourage fleas. Actually dull purple would be a better way to describe its flowers. It is about 30 cm tall, has long narrow leaves, and is not very prominent. It flowers in July and August.

The last of this group of wild flower specialities is the haresfoot clover. One of the easiest to identify of all of the clovers, it has flowers in heads at the ends of stalks, and they look like fluffy rabbit or hare's feet. They are pink and white, and quite pretty when fully open. Typical of sandy heathland and grassland, these five represent a plant community that is rare in England as a whole, and almost unique in Northamptonshire. All the more tragic therefore, if they are lost to us as a result of the expansion of the town.

Corn Marigold

DELAPRE PARK

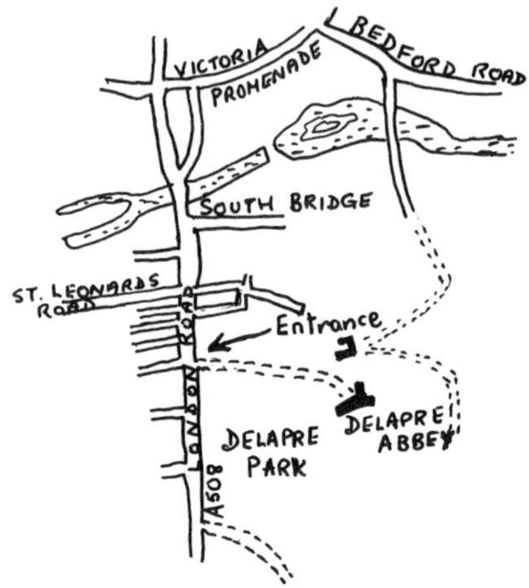

Take the London Road, and less than a mile from the town centre, turn left into the park, and drive to the parking area in front of the manor house.

The town is blessed with several lovely parks, and some would say this is the finest of them all. On an autumn morning, with the trees showing all the colours from reds, oranges, and russets, through to fading greens and yellows, and with a wraith of mist curling over the grass from the river nearby, it is a scene which is hard to match.

Pass the front of the house, walking to the right. After a hundred metres a small entrance leads into the former walled kitchen garden, bright from spring until autumn with colourful flowers. A door at the bottom right leads into the planted woodland. The borders against the walls have a good collection of hydrangeas, and other interesting garden plants like the spindle called 'Silver queen', and winter sweet, known to botanists as *Chimonanthus*.

The trees are all planted, and there are a host of species, many of them exotic and quite rare. They include Wellingtonia, the yellow-berried and weeping varieties of holly, and witch hazel. At the edge of the lawn is a great tulip tree, related to the magnolias, with curious four-lobed leaves, deeply notched at the tip, and quite unlike those of any other tree. In June and July its flowers appear, vaguely tulip-shaped, and shaded with orange, green, and cream. Before they fall the leaves change first to yellow, and then gradually to crimson. A native of North America, its wood - known as whitewood - is used for house interiors, and a heart stimulant has been extracted from its bark.

In the shrubbery there is a contorted variety of the hazel, which has been called corkscrew hazel or Harry Lauder's walking stick tree. The knobbly twisting and turning walking stick, the trade mark of the old music-hall comedian, is mirrored in the way the branches and twigs curve first one way, and then the other, as if the tree cannot make up its mind which way to grow. Its contorted growth is due to the fact that the branches grow faster on one side than the other, and then suddenly change to grow faster on the opposite side. Even the catkins in springtime are twisted in this odd fashion. Truly a freak among trees.

[At the heart of this woodland there is a little 'secret' low-walled area, with a pool, almost totally shaded by tall trees, where luxuriant hart's-tongue ferns grow. Generally you would have to go to the west country to find them as large as they are here, because they thrive best where the rainfall is high, and the air is moist and mild. Here they are protected from drying out by the trees around them, with the stonework providing them with the crevices in which they grow well. Turn the long strap-shaped leaves over to find pale green oblong patches on the backs; in autumn they are a rusty colour. These are the spores, dust-fine to be carried long distances on the breeze, to find new places in which to grow.]

We have bracketed the foregoing passage because a change has occurred leading to the near-extermination of the hart's-tongue ferns. When working on the nearby golf course, the pipe that fed the little stream into the gardens was broken, the grotto has dried out, and the plants have died through lack of moisture. We have left the paragraph in as a reminder that in a man-made environment change is continuous, and communities of plants and animals are constantly at risk.

Just a few metres away is an open area where hundreds of daffodils turn their heads to the sun to catch the welcome warmth in early spring. As the rich yellow of their blooms begins to fade, the patch of unmown grass left for their sake is enlivened by the delicate clear white of meadow saxifrage, a plant usually found only in old pasture or grassy woodland rides. Uncommon in Northamptonshire it survives here only because the grass is left uncut until later in the season, for the sake of the daffodils.

Now walk through the wood, away from the house, to the far end where there is an embryo woodland, planted by the Mayor of Northampton and others in 1989 to celebrate the 800th anniversary of the granting of the towns' charter by King Richard I. As yet the trees have not grown large enough to attract woodland birds, although goldfinches, greenfinches, and chaffinches sing in them, and build their nests there. The way that the ground undulates shows that this is ancient 'ridge and furrow' land, formed when the medieval ox-drawn plough passed to and fro.

Continue walking and you will soon arrive at the large lake, which is a flooded gravel-pit. A path leads all the way around it, parts of which may be under water in winter. Although the Northampton Water-ski Club has its headquarters here, some birds tolerate the disturbance very well. Coots, all-black with a white beak and shield on the forehead, call constantly to one another, and argue furiously over their territories, with much splashing about in the water. Platform nests of dead reeds hold stone-coloured, black speckled eggs. The fluffy black chicks have yellow around the neck, with red beak and forehead. Many of them do not survive for very long, being taken by a variety of land-based predators like foxes and stoats. Perhaps most fearsome of them all is the pike which steals silently up from the watery depths to snatch them from the surface.

At the far end of the lake, away from the water-ski course, a pair of great crested grebes may be found. A hundred years ago this was one of our most endangered birds. The craze for its feathers, worn as a fashion accessory by Victorian ladies, led to it being almost exterminated. Today, under protection and aided by our flooded gravel pits and reservoirs, it has become one of our more familiar and well-loved waterbirds, with some 8000 individuals counted in England and Wales. A lovely, graceful bird it swims low in the water, sometimes with its back almost awash, and ever-ready to slip

Great crested grebe

quietly beneath the surface with scarcely a ripple if danger threatens or to fish. Its dagger-shaped beak is, like that of the kingfisher, the mark of a fish-eater. The stripey youngsters may sometimes be seen hitching a lift, hidden among the feathers of the parent's back.

Plants of the water margin include branched bur-reed with globular yellowish flower-heads, followed by spiky seed-cases. At other times the sword-shaped leaves of this plant are distinctive. Oval leaves lying flat upon the water's surface are of the broad-leaved pondweed, which is common in lakes and ponds all over Britain. Turn over some of these leaves carefully and you may find water snails, including the coiled-up ramshorns. Clusters of greenish or transparent jelly sticking to the leaves are the snail's eggs. Other marginal plants include persicaria, with deep pink flower spikes, and the water plantain, with pointed oval leaves, and tall flower spikes. Canadian pondweed, with translucent green leaves attached to the stem in groups of three, is common in the shallow waters of the lake. The tranquillity of the lake contrasts with the bustle of the surrounding area. Industry is all around, with the continuous roar of the traffic on the Nene Valley Way ever-present.

EASTFIELD PARK

The Park can be reached from several points between the main Kettering Road, and Booth Lane North.

Much of this land once belonged to the Manfield Family. Moses Philip Manfield, the boot and shoe factory magnate, built and lived in the great house, on the Kettering Road, which later became the orthopaedic hospital, and as I write languishes empty and vandalised. It was June when I last visited the park. The weather was pleasantly warm and everything was still green and shimmering in a slight heat haze. Students from the nearby colleges, taking a break from their classes, relaxed on the grass, and occasional snatches of lazy conversation reached me on the still air. Mothers with their infants from the nearby estates played or strolled around the lake.

As I skirted the long strip of woodland the sweet full song of the blackcap - the 'poor man's nightingale' of country folk - drifted down to me. The mellow tones of blackbird and a song thrush provided a background of bird music that almost, though never quite, threatened to drown out the roar from the town. A dunnock started into stuttered song as I passed along. The peevish alarm calls of the great spotted woodpecker could be heard in the distance.

In the understorey of the woodland there are many field maples, the native 'sycamore' that is infinitely more lovely than its more widespread cousin. Some of these in the nearby grassland were obviously planted by man. A big ash tree intrigued me: it sprouted several huge branches from very low down, but I was unable to decide whether it had once been coppiced - cut from the base to encourage a crop of poles - or whether it was a survivor from a hedgerow that had long since disappeared.

Although the lake has suffered badly both from silting up and from litter dumping in the past, there is still a wealth of interesting plants around its margin, together with the wildlife associated with it. With stems well over two metres long, the pendulous sedge is a spectacular plant which I usually associate with Salcey Forest, although the textbooks tell us it also occurs on river banks where there is plenty of shade. Here it is probably introduced, but thrives at the lake edge, as if nature had intended it should be there. It looks like an enormous grass plant, but it can easily be distinguished by its triangular stems. Those of grasses or rushes are round or oval. When in full flower it is a beautiful plant with its long grass-like leaves. The flower-spike is tipped with the male flowers which, when ripe, are bright yellow with pollen, and looking like the bushy tail of some exotic mammal. Beneath are the female flowers, long drooping cylinders of green with a purplish tinge. Another plant with grass-like leaves is the yellow flag iris, which brightens up the marginal vegetation with its large clear yellow blooms on tall stems, and surrounded by leaves like green upright swords. Later on, as its seed-pods ripen they spin open to reveal large brown seeds. These have corky air-filled tissues, enabling them to float off on the water to colonise pastures new. In days gone by country folk valued its long acrid root as a cure for toothache. A black dye was also made from it, which was used as ink. And if that wasn't enough it was dried and ground to make snuff, and its seeds were roasted for coffee.

Pendulus sedge

Also flourishing was the tufted vetch which had fastened its questing tendrils on to the surrounding plants to scramble into the sunlight. Its deep blue flowers, typical of the pea family, were gathered into spikes 10 cms or more long, making a brave splash of colour at the lakeside. Although generally thought of as a plant of hedgerow or thicket, in my experience it grows best of all where it has its feet in the damp soil.

Although these were in evidence the dominant plants of the water margin were the two species of reed, the reed canary grass, and the common reed, also known as the Norfolk reed. It was from the latter that I heard the sound of familiar birdsong. Hard to describe, it was at times a pleasant musical warbling, at others a guttural grating. This was the reed warbler, closely linked to the Norfolk reed, which is where it prefers to nest. To the birdwatcher this is a typical 'little brown job', and it is mainly brown and grey with no prominent markings to speak of. Add to this the fact that it often prefers to hide in the dense plant growth, from which it scolds the observer with harsh calls, and we have a bird that is something of an enigma. Part of the puzzle is how to tell it from its close relative the sedge warbler, which I also saw and heard here. When a good view is possible the streaked head pattern and 'scaly' back feathering separates the sedge from the featureless reed species. And the song of the sedge has more harsh notes than the reed, although I would be hard put to tell an indifferent reed warbler from a good sedge warbler by its song!

Reed warbler

Both species come to Northamptonshire as summer residents, their winter homes being in tropical Africa. The reed warbler makes a very deep cup-shaped nest, skilfully attached to several reed stems, often where there is 30 cms or more of water. This gives it some protection from the attentions of land-based predators. The nest has to be deep to stop the eggs from falling out when high winds sweep the lake shore, bending the reeds almost flat before it. It may be protected from four-footed predators, but it is very vulnerable to the cuckoo. In some parts of the country pairs of reed warblers play unwilling hosts to the cuckoo.

As may be expected there was the usual gang of mallards, many of them with downy ducklings, as well as Canada geese, also with well-grown young, ever-ready to swarm around on the promise of a few handfuls of bread. On the edge of this milling crowd were moorhens and coots, ready to nip in and snatch their share of the meal. Often they too, had their fluffy youngsters in tow. After the excitement has died down, the few forgotten scraps of bread are bunted about by small fishes as they attempt to swallow bite-sized pieces. Their task was made easier as the crusts became softened by the water.

Common tern

Another pleasant surprise was the sudden appearance over the lake of the graceful common tern, perhaps a wanderer from the gravel pits along the Nene Valley, or from Sywell Country Park. It nests in both places. It swept easily from one end of the lake to the other. Every so often it paused and hovered, and peered intently downward before dropping to seize a small fish in its beak. Obviously a parent with hungry young to feed, and having gathered a respectable catch it flew swiftly off. In a few weeks time, as autumn approaches, it and its young will leave us for winter quarters off the coast of tropical Africa. Only in the past decade or so has it made its summer home in Northamptonshire, attracted by the chain of gravel pits, where it nests on shingly islets, or increasingly on purpose-built rafts anchored in deep water, as at Sywell.

THORNTON'S PARK

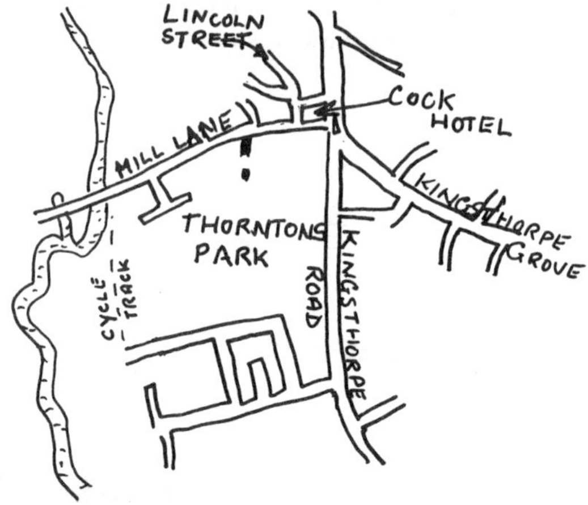

Leave Northampton town centre on the A508 Market Harborough road. After about 3.5km look for Thornton's Park, on the left and surrounded by a low stone wall. Turn left at the traffic lights at the Cock Hotel junction, then first right to park in Lincoln Street. The entrance to the park is almost opposite, in Mill Lane.

The solidly square hall and its gardens are in front of you to the right. Built in about 1795 for the wealthy Thornton family, it became public property when it was acquired by Northampton Corporation. Today the hall serves as a community centre, and the park and gardens are a quiet haven for the town-dweller, with a variety of interesting trees, shrubs, and herbaceous plants. The gardens are surrounded by a ha-ha, which is a sunken wall and ditch designed to keep out livestock without obstructing the view from the house. A huge Chile pine, or monkey puzzle tree, may be seen on the left of the entrance to the gardens. An impressive cedar of Lebanon stands opposite the door to the hall, with two Spanish or sweet chestnuts nearby. The park is home to a variety of common birds, including mistle and song thrushes, greenfinches and chaffinches. Grey squirrels are often seen here.

On the manicured grassland a mistle thrush may often be seen hopping about. Tall and bold with grey-brown upper-parts and creamy black-spotted breast, it is worth spending some time watching, as it searches for food. This is a much larger bird than the golden-brown song thrush that flings its beautiful music into the morning or evening sky, and it makes itself heard even above the roar of the traffic. The mistle thrush also has a lovely, but quite different, song, with gentle phrases of only a few notes. Similar to the blackbird, it lacks the variety of the master singer. Folklore dubs the mistle thrush the *stormcock*, because it is said to sing its song from the treetop even into the teeth of a gale, but I find the bird wiser than that. He chooses to sing his best song on a fine, still early spring morning, perhaps when the grass is grizzled with overnight hoar frost.

Mistle thrush

KINGSTHORPE MILL LOCAL NATURE RESERVE

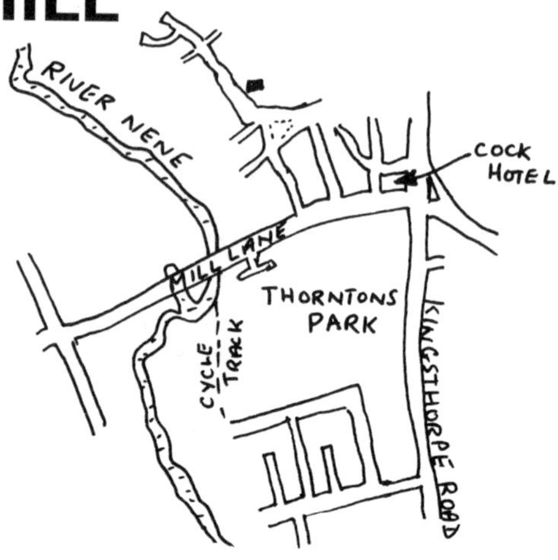

To reach the Kingsthorpe Mill Local Nature Reserve, walk to the lower end of Thornton's Park, cross over the footpath, and a stile takes you into the reserve area.

The Reserve, on either side of Mill Lane, straddles the Brampton arm of the River Nene. Made up of a number of fields, which are grazed by local horses, there is a network of hedges and a number of ponds and river channels. Hay is taken from some of the grasslands in late summer, all of which are still prone to flooding, although this happens infrequently now due to drainage works.

Before the modern busy road was built there was a public bathing pool here, which closed in about 1940. The site of the old red brick and stone watermill, from which the Reserve takes its name, could still be found, until it was buried by the road. Only the mill race, now partly filled in, remains.

The meadows that you pass through as you make your way towards the road bridge, are full of wild flowers during the warmer months. As well as buttercups and daisies, look out for the uncommon pignut, which will only thrive in undisturbed grassland. It gets its name from the edible nut-like tuber that it hides underground. The wild flowers attract butterflies like the meadow brown and small heath, and you may also catch the bright flash of blue as a male common blue flies past. The female is mainly dull brown in colour with just a powdering of blue scales at the base of the wings, and so is harder to find.

Pass under the road bridge to take the right-hand bank leading upstream. Bridges and a boardwalk take you over the streams and a marshy patch. About a hundred metres along the bank is a group of white poplar trees. The name comes from the leaves, which are green above with felted white undersides. In winter the dark grey-green trunks stand out. To the right there is a small pool, once part of the mill race, with water starwort and flote-grass growing over its surface.

To the right the scrub and willow tree lined bank of the mill race is very attractive to birds in the winter. These include the redwing and fieldfare, two relatives of the thrush which migrate south to these parts from Scandinavia. The redwing is like a small dark song thrush with a patch of brick-red feathers on its sides and under the wings; the fieldfare is longer than a blackbird with pale grey head and rump, and chestnut back. It has a distinctive chattering call-note. About 400 metres upstream there is a flat field on which the pattern of an old water meadow system may be traced. These were formerly common along rivers and streams. By means of a herringbone pattern of shallow ditches they were deliberately flooded every winter. The silt from the flood waters enriched the soil, and when they were drained in spring the rapid lush growth of grass yielded high-quality grazing or hay. But they needed a lot of maintenance, and this is why almost all of them have fallen into disuse. Changes in agricultural practices are an added reason for their decline.

A few yards from the river is the low embankment which retained the flood water. Around the edge of the meadow runs the dyke which carried water from a spring on the hillside above. On the meadow itself the shallow drainage channels can still be made out, especially when the ground is frosty, or the sun is low on the horizon.

Lady's bedstraw

This water meadow still supports some of the attractive wild flowers of wetlands, although annually they decrease in numbers. Lady's smock and the spectacular marsh marigold, known around here as *mollyblobs*, are at their best in spring. A few plants of the rare meadow saxifrage, with showy white flowers, may still be found. A little later in the year small numbers of the exquisite rose-pink flowers of ragged robin occur around the edges of the field, where they are joined by the hayrattle with its yellow flowers. The latter is what the botanist calls a hemi-parasite; to you and me a semi-parasite. Although its roots seem capable of seeking out their own nutriment from the soil, it seizes every opportunity to fasten its roots on to other plants and steal food from them. Lady's bedstraw, with its distinctive hay-like smell, and honey-scented flowers, is in bloom in July and August. It has legendary associations with the infant Jesus, where it was supposed to have been used in the manger, and in days gone by it was dried and, together with other plants, was used as a mattress. The flowers were also collected and used to curdle milk, and a red dye was extracted from the stems.

The hedges are important providing a refuge for a variety of small mammals, which find cover in the hedge bottoms. The sparrowhawk is well aware of this, and can often be seen patrolling the area when it is in need of a meal.

Many years ago, when this was still a wild and remote spot, known locally as Kingsthorpe Moors, the meadow used to ring to the cries of the redshank and snipe, both of which nested here. They are long gone as are most of the skylarks and the yellow wagtails, and we are the poorer for not having them.

In the muddy stretches of the river the broad arrow-shaped leaves of arrowhead, held on stiff stems, may be found during the summer. Its clear three-petalled white flowers have a purple blotch at the base. It has two types of leaves: those which grow below the surface are long and ribbon-like, able to yield to the slightest current. Those above have the distinctive arrow-shape, from which the plant was named. In winter it dies back to thick stems under the mud, where the plant is busy, producing the buds from which new plants grow. It has flowers which are either male or female, both being produced on the same plant. One old book says that 'its root is most nutritious, and might well be used in this country as food; in warmer climates where the whole plant is more luxuriant, its large size renders it very valuable'.

In the pools, the occasional flash of silver from the gloomy depths are signs of big fish such as roach and chub, a sight to quicken the pulse of the angler. Here the yellow waterlily threatens to cover the surface with its waxy green leaves, some of them as large as dinner plates. Country folk called it 'brandy bottle' because its yellow flowers give off a smell not unlike that of stale brandy and later, when the seed capsules form, they bear an uncanny resemblance to miniature bottles of spirits. Turn the leaves over and the under surface is likely to have a number of water snails like the great ramshorn, and the great pond snail - the latter shaped like a whelk. Strips or blobs of jelly with greyish dots are often present: these are the snails' eggs. Leeches also attach themselves to the underside of the leaves.

Not many years ago the sprightly water vole was common along these banks; the plop as it dived into the water and the V-shaped wake as it swam across to the other bank were familiar sights and sounds. Today all are gone, part of a worrying national decline, said by some to be due to the predatory introduced mink, although I believe there are other factors at work.

Three-spined stickleback

Beneath the water's glassy surface the fish of our childhood may still be found. Patrolling in shoals, the three-spined sticklebacks are on the lookout for anything edible. These 5 cms long flashes of quicksilver have barbed fins that can pierce the skin and draw blood from the fingers if handled carelessly. In summer the males take over a small area by the water margin, which becomes their territory, and which they fiercely defend. They become handsome creatures, with blood red chests and bellies and iridescent blue and green scales. They build nests from pieces of waterweed, glued together by threads secreted from the kidneys.

Using a special display the male attracts several females to the nest, and drives them in by the front entrance. Once inside they lay their eggs, and then leave by the back. He enters the nest and fertilises them. After mating, each female is driven away by the male, and plays no further part in looking after eggs and young. While the eggs are developing, the male constantly fans a current of fresh water over them, and throws out any that go mouldy. After the fry have hatched he becomes the ideal devoted father, making sure they all stay together, gently gathering up any strays in his mouth, and blowing them back into the nest.

LINGS WOOD LOCAL NATURE RESERVE

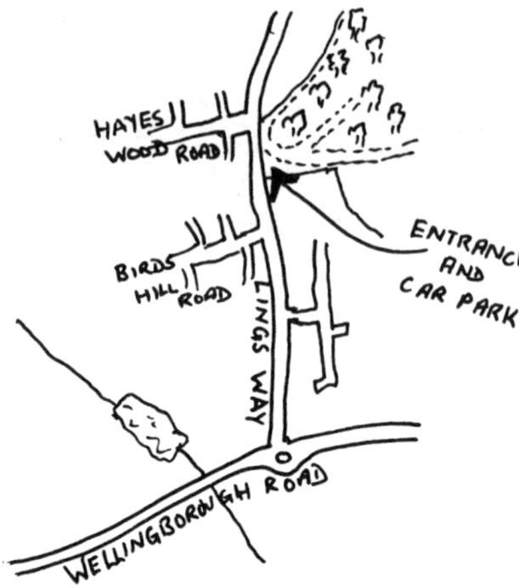

To reach Lings Wood, leave the town along the Wellingborough Road. After 7km turn left at the mini-roundabout - about 1km past the West Favell centre (on your left) signposted Lings and this takes you into Lings Way. About 1km along this road look for a sign which indicates Northamptonshire Wildlife Trust. This leads into a small car park. It is easier if you leave your car here. Follow the track to the right and then take the left track up towards the white house hidden among the trees

This is the Headquarters of the Wildlife Trust for Northamptonshire, part of a Wildlife Trust group which includes Bedfordshire and Cambridgeshire. Here the staff work tirelessly for wildlife conservation within the county, and to safeguard the nature reserves entrusted to their care.

It is hard now to recall that only a little more than a quarter of a century ago Northampton ended with nothing but green fields beyond the Westone estate. At that time Lings Wood was still privately owned, and it seemed a remote and secret place. I used to drive my green double-decker bus along the Wellingborough road, where smug-looking, over-dressed male pheasants were commoner than cars. How different things are today, and yet Lings Wood remains as a valuable habitat for wildlife, all the more important because it stands on a soil type that has all-but disappeared from the county.

Lings Wood is one area which the Wildlife Trust manages. In the sixteenth century it was a wild place, covered with heather and gorse, and dotted with clumps of silver birch. The commoners grazed their beasts on the stretches of open grassland. Most of the trees seen today were planted not that many years ago. The underlying soil is what is known as a podsol. Here a light sandy soil is covered with a very acid layer of decaying plant matter. Beneath the sand is the hard pan, which is sometimes so thick and solid that even thrusting tree roots cannot find a way through it.

This kind of soil was once found in a broad band across the centre of the county from beyond Harpole in the southwest to Overstone and Sywell in the northeast. The area where Kingsthorpe Cemetery and the Obelisk estate are today was on this starved podsol soil. In late Victorian times it was a wild lonely landscape, and a place of escape as recently as my own boyhood in the 1940's. Dear old John Clare sought refuge on Helpston Heath, near Peterborough, which was close to his home, and very similar to Lings Wood.

Today, Lings Wood has only remnants of the original heathland plants. As the trees have begun to close in so the herb layer has died out, leaving only the occasional clump of broad buckler-fern, which puts forth its dark green shepherd's crooks of new leaves in the spring. Where a little more light filters through, bracken carpets the woodland floor, ready to slash to the bone the flesh of the unwary who would try to pull it up. Its wiry fronds grow to over two metres tall in places, over-topping even the willow herbs and straggly brambles that grow with it. The conifers here are Scots pine, Douglas fir, Norway spruce and larch. The first three are evergreens, but the larch turns first yellow then rust-coloured in autumn, before shedding its needles like its broad-leafed neighbours. All of these are alien species, not found naturally around here, and the evergreen rhododendron that grows beneath them is another non-native. Introduced from Asia in the eighteenth century, it has spread widely where there are acid soils. In May and June it puts on a spectacular show of flowers. But from the conservationists point of view it is not a good plant to have around. It spreads quickly smothering other plants, and not many birds or other wildlife find a use for it. Although the delightful plant will be left along the footpaths, the Trust is attempting to clear large areas. Where it forms 'blanket' cover, it excludes other plants. In one area which has been cleared the Trust is re-establishing the traditional heathland which, as we have already said, once covered much of the area, and from which the term 'Lings' has come.

Any area left will grow out of control, and Lings Wood is no exception. To keep a balance, the Trust carries out management work, and clearing areas of rhododendrons is one method. Another is to coppice certain trees. This is a traditional method for managing woodland for timber production. Some trees, like hazel and sycamore, are cut down close to the ground. The tree doesn't die, but instead sends up a number of new shoots which grow into trunks. These produce a shrubby area, in which some trees will be left to grow 'naturally'. Areas of wood like this are known as coppice with standards.

In other areas, trees were often planted too close together. When they grow up, they prevent light from reaching the ground, and the plants can no longer survive. By thinning such areas the Trust hopes to encourage a greater diversity of wildlife. For many years Lings Wood was 'neglected', and during that time many of the older trees became

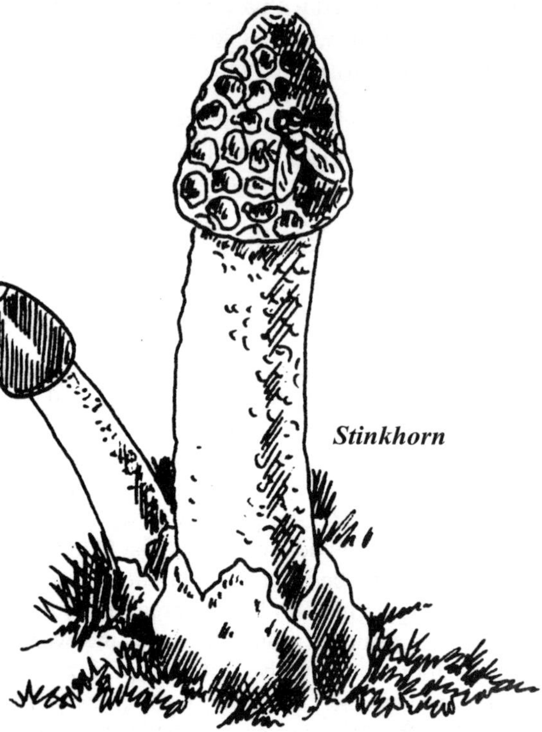

Stinkhorn

dangerous. By felling some of these trees glades are opened up, which encourages a variety of wildlife. Some of the timber will be left, since rotting wood is valuable to a range of wildlife. In contrast to this, other areas of woodland will be left to 'nature' without any interference from the Trust.

If you are in Lings Wood any time from May onwards it may not be long before you become aware of a strong smell like rotting meat, perhaps coming from the bracken or from bushes close at hand. Look around and you will find the stinkhorn, one of the oddest of all the fungi. It looks a bit like a dull white candle with a cap which, when fresh, is khaki-coloured, and it is from this sticky mess that the evil smell comes. This revolting odour is irresistible to carrion eating flies, and they land in droves to eat it. Some of it sticks to their hairy bodies, and as they later walk about the woodland floor it rubs off, with its complement of spores. Eventually individual spores may germinate to grow into the new generation of stinkhorns. The growth of this fungus is remarkable. First a white sphere, about 6 cms or so across appears on the ground, pushing aside the leafy carpet to reach the light. In folklore these are 'witches eggs', so-called because if split open they reveal the same slimy mess that later coats the cap. In cold weather they may remain at this stage for days or even weeks. But given a warm spell the sphere bursts and within hours the long white stem and spore-laden cap has grown. In a short time, its aim of reproduction accomplished, the cap and stem collapse, leaving nothing to show for this remarkable process.

There are birds of many species within the woodland. In addition to the usual blackbirds, thrushes, chaffinches, crows, magpies, and wood pigeons, there are several warblers that come here to breed every summer, having spent the winter in Africa. They include the willow warbler and chiffchaff, two little greenish-grey birds that look so similar that even expert birdwatchers find it hard to tell them apart. Fortunately their songs are totally different, the willow warbler having a short but very sweet song, a series of clear notes cascading down the scale; whereas the chiffchaff has just two notes, enough to repeat its name over and over again 'chiff-chaff, chiff-chaff, chiff-chaff'. To some it is monotonous, but to me it is a sound of summer, and a woodland without it churning away in the background would be unthinkable.

All three of the British woodpeckers are found here. Listen out for the ringing laugh of the green woodpecker, also known in country districts as yaffle. Largest of the group, it is about the same size as a jackdaw. Mainly green and yellow, with some red and black about the head, it is a handsome bird. Like the others of its group it clings to the tree trunk with large strong feet, using the stiffened feathers of its tail pressed against the trunk as a kind of third limb. It drills a hole into a branch, about the size of a tennis ball, and makes a cavity where the white eggs are laid. This is such a desirable residence, in bird terms, that starlings often oust the woodpeckers, to nest and raise their own young. The green woodpecker may often be disturbed from the ground, where it searches for ants, a favourite food.

Green woodpecker

The other two species of woodpecker are both mainly black-and-white. A great deal of mis-information is found in the bird guides as to how to tell them apart. They may be separated on size alone. The great spotted species is the size of a song thrush, while the lesser spotted is great tit sized. The larger species is much the commoner of the two, advertising its presence with strident 'chick-chick' calls of alarm, or by its loud drumming on a hollow branch. Observers reckon that they 'tap' their beaks on the branch up to 20 times a second - some 1200 times a minute! The lesser spotted woodpecker also drums. This is the way they advertise their presence to other woodpeckers. The entrance to the nest is about 5.5 cms across, while the lesser spotted measures about 3.8 cms. Woodpeckers prefer to drill their holes in dead wood, where beetle grubs and other wood-boring insects are found.

There are butterflies too in Lings Wood. You may expect to see species like the brimstone, green-veined white, and orange-tip feasting on the nectar of spring flowers. The first two also occur again later in the summer, when they are joined by meadow browns and gatekeepers. Lovely names some of these creatures have, haven't they? In a good year two or three of them may be seen crowding together with bees and hoverflies on the same yarrow flower head. The speckled wood is also found here, a true woodland sprite as you would expect from its name, although its caterpillar feeds on various tall grasses found along the rides. When freshly emerged the adult is a deep chocolate brown on the upperwings, flecked with clear yellow. As it sits on the ground or in low vegetation, the yellow looks like tiny points of sunlight as they filter through the tracery of twigs above - excellent camouflage. Not spectacular, but a very pretty insect.

Badgers used to be found in Lings Wood, but they have succumbed to the pressure of the surrounding housing development. What is certain is that the secretive muntjac or barking deer still lives here. Not long ago I glimpsed a female with her half-grown fawn during a walk at first light. She seemed in no hurry as she trotted along one of the tracks, before leading her young one into the safety of the deep green bracken. The occasional fox may be seen here too, no doubt attracted by the rabbits which still manage to survive despite frequent poaching.

But it is the grey squirrels that are the most prominent and easily watched of the mammals. In autumn they may be seen scampering along the ground, attracted by the harvest of fallen nuts and seeds, and at other times searching for roots and succulent shoots. As summer draws on, and the cones begin to swell with their precious seeds on the pine trees, you may stand below and listen to the regular pattering as discarded cones drop through the branches, the seeds having been eaten by the squirrels. Often twenty or more grey squirrels will be feeding in the trees, the falling cones being the only sign of their presence, as they stuff themselves to bursting point on the nutritious kernels.

Grey squirrel

Although the western part of Lings Wood is on sandy soil, an abrupt change takes place close to Lings House to a much heavier soil. Here, too, there is a small pond where visiting school children go dipping for the invertebrates (minibeasts) that live there. In summer damselflies, and sometimes the larger dragonflies are seen, hawking the air close by, in search of their small insect prey. Their grotesque carnivorous nymphs live hidden away among the tangle of weeds in the pond.

There is something to interest the visitor to Lings Wood at any time of year. Yet it is entirely a man-made wood, planted by our forefathers in the recent past, to change for ever the original wild heathland.

THE RIVER NENE

UPTON MILL TO DUSTON MILL MEADOW

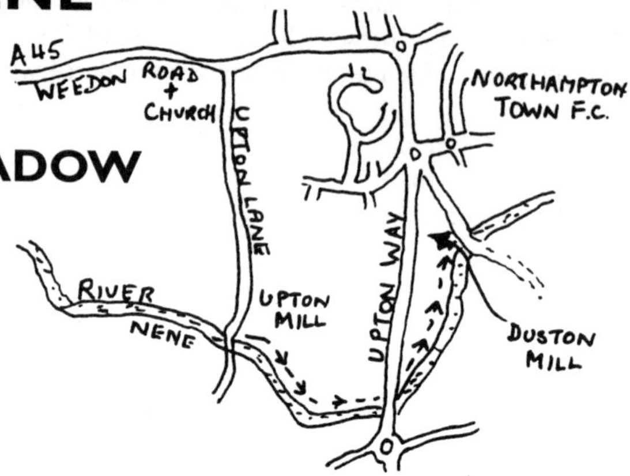

The River Nene walks start at Upton Mill, on edge of Northampton and can be reached from the lane off the A45, and next to Upton Church. The walk of about 1 mile follows sign posts along the Nene Way.

A rough estimate suggests that there may be around 20 kilometres or more of river bank as the Nene and its tributaries wind their way through the town, and it is possible to walk the banks of most of them. The River Nene enters Northampton at Upton, having risen between Staverton and Badby on the western edge of the county. At Upton the Wootton Brook flows into it, surprisingly having its source at Horton to the east of the town. Near South Bridge, and to the rear of the Carlsberg brewery, it is joined by the Brampton Brook, which rises at Naseby in the north. The latter is 'fuelled' by a second tributary of the River Nene These, together with several kilometres of canal bank, provide many delightful waterside walks, each with an abundance of wildlife (and historical) interest, together with the seclusion that many of us look for.

Both the river and the canal flow along the valley at Upton, passing the giant Sixfields entertainment and sports complex as they do so. There are worked out gravel pits which provide homes for a wide range of aquatic wildlife. A rare winter visitor here has been the yellow-and-black billed whooper swan. a 'stranger in the camp' causing consternation among the local red-and-black billed mute swans. Redshanks that once nested in the marshy fields here have now gone, and they are a great loss to wildlife enthusiasts. Less than a mile away towards Kislingbury the spectacular curlew formerly bred. Both species are casualties of the rapid expansion of this part of the town in the recent past.

I remember being down here one murky January day when the place was shrouded in thick grey mist. Everywhere seemed cloaked in silence too, when suddenly out of the gloom a short-eared owl appeared above my head, and only a few feet away. The owl was as startled to see me, as I was to see it; it veered off to one side, to be swallowed up once more by the almost impenetrable mist. For me a treasured split-second encounter the memory of which has not been dimmed by the passage of time.

Along this stretch of both the river and the canal, turn over some of the huge waterlily leaves and you may reveal the uncommon river snail. This large species somewhat resembles the garden snail, and like it it is a herbivore, browsing on blanket weed and other types of algae. Most water snails, like the freshwater whelk, need to come to the surface to take in supplies of oxygen, but this one has gills which it uses to extract oxygen. Another difference is that the females retain their eggs within the shell until they hatch, with some fifty tiny replicas of the adult appearing at a time. River snails have a horny trapdoor attached to the foot, which they can 'slam shut' if danger threatens.

Ramshorn snail

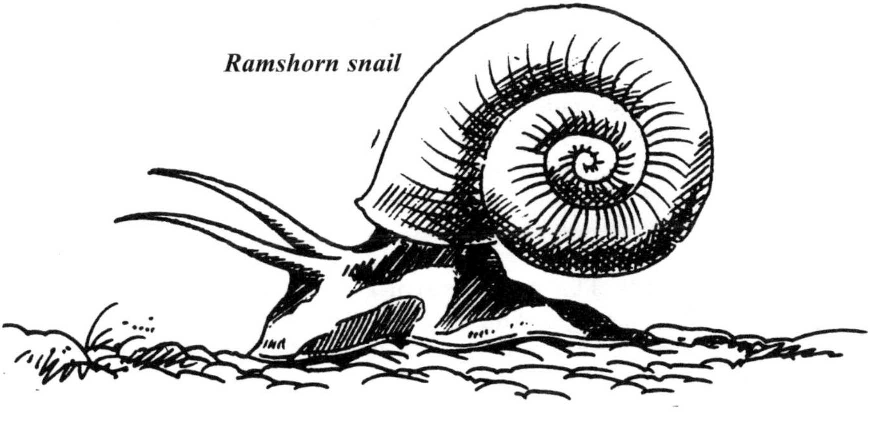

The great ramshorn snail is also found here. Quite a local species it is not found in many stretches of the river. It prefers hard slow-flowing or still water, with plenty of weed growth. According to the books its shell may be up to 30 mm wide, but I found one some years ago that measured 37 mm across its shell. Every now and then a bright crimson specimen turns up, instead of the usual velvety brown. An albino, it lacks any body pigment, which allows the red blood to show through. Old specimens are often covered with water moss growth, and are well camouflaged. Having photographed one of these, I was astonished to find that when I looked closely at the picture, a small ramshorn snail had found the perfect hiding place, in a depression in the shell of the larger snail. Although it was tempting to think of them as father and son - or mother and daughter - the two were of different species.

THE RIVER NENE

DUSTON MILL MEADOW NATURE RESERVE

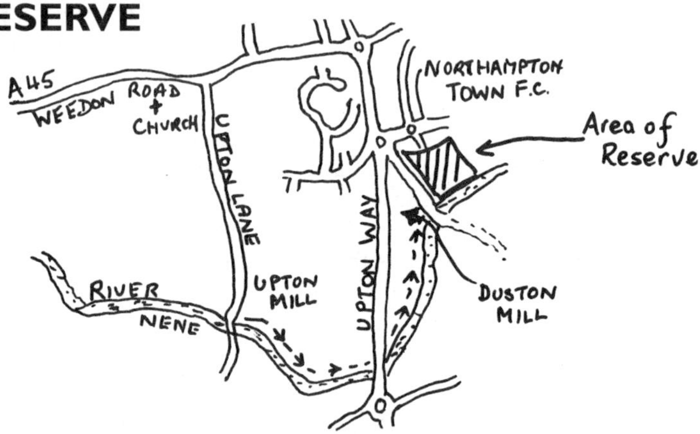

Duston Mill Meadow is a small Wildlife Trust Reserve situated to the south of the Sixfields Entertainment Complex. Access can be gained from either of the two roundabouts near the Sixfields complex, or from the layby along the A45 between the Sixfields and A508/A45 roundabout.

The Reserve consists of 0.8 ha (2 acres) of wet grassland with some ancient ridge and furrow. Particularly good for sedges, at least seven species have been recorded. They include the glaucous, hairy and greater pond sedge. In spring the field is bright with the pale lilac blooms of the cuckoo flower, so called because they appear at about the same time as the cuckoo. In Northampton district it is much better known as lady's smock, the upturned flower looking like the full skirts of the old milkmaids in another of its many folklore names. A member of the cabbage family, its leaves taste a little like radish. The lovely orange tip butterfly uses it as the food plant for its caterpillar, along with the garlic mustard, which is common in the hedgerows around here. If you have ever tried to keep up with a flying orange-tip you will know that it is a very rapid flier. And when it does settle, often amid the flowers of keck, or Queen Anne's lace as it is also known, it seems to 'vanish'. This is because although the male is creamy white with orange tips to the upper wings (the female lacks the orange tips), the underside has a chequered pattern of green and white; perfect camouflage when it lands on the flowers. Because this butterfly depends upon flower-rich meadows it has become less common in recent years.

Later on the area is patrolled by numerous dragonflies and damselflies. They include the big brown hawker, with wings that rustle as it flies rapidly to and fro on the look-out for its insect prey; and the red or brown bodied common and ruddy darters. To mark the boundaries of two sides of the Reserve there are newly-planted hedges. Once established these will be managed to provide good nesting and feeding opportunities for birds, as well as for small mammals. Formerly used by Duston Mill, there is an old channel which flows past the reserve on its southern side. Many willows grow here, marking the position of a one-time osier bed which provided wands for the village basket-maker. So the reserve lays in the centre of a fascinating area for wildlife. Downstream, closer to town, Storton's Pits are being developed into a new nature reserve which will incorporate a 10 acre reedbed, all thanks to the great help of Pioneer Aggregates.

THE RIVER NENE

SOUTH BRIDGE TO WEST BRIDGE

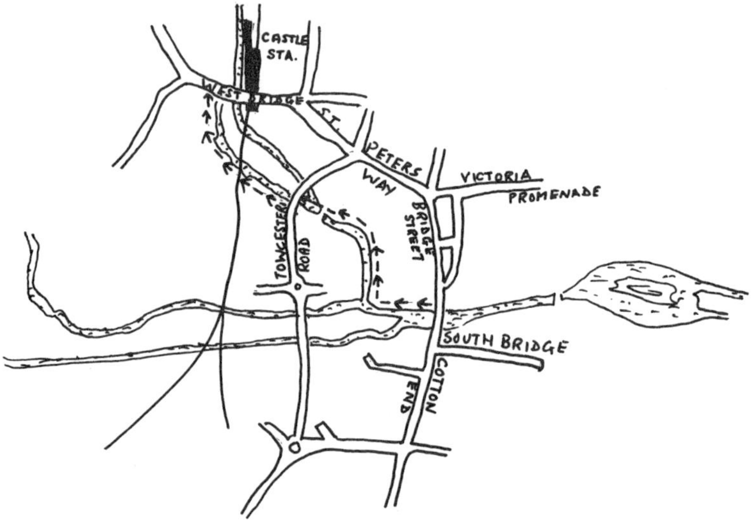

South Bridge is on Bridge Street, .5 mile (1km) south of the town centre. Either park in a car park or a nearby street.

Despite the occasional serious pollution incident and poor water quality from time to time in the river and its tributaries where they flow through the town, there is still much of wildlife interest to discover. The walk from South Bridge through to West Bridge, by the railway station, is particularly rewarding. The paved area close to, and upstream of, South Bridge is where the Crown Maltings of 1803, an impressive waterfront building, once stood, and which should have been saved as part of our heritage. During the summer the water's surface here is covered with the waxy leaves and yellow flowers of waterlilies - once referred to as 'brandy-bottles' by our ancestors. The reed-fringed banks have yellow flag irises, purple-spiked marsh wound-wort, and the square-stemmed water betony, which is also known as figwort because its seed-pods resemble tiny figs.

Many trees have been planted along the banks, but sallow, willow and buddleia have all managed to intrude. Where the path skirts the old gasworks site there is a great thicket of Japanese knotweed which is nearly 3 metres high in summer. The old concrete roads have biting stonecrop, with its bright yellow star-shaped flowers, and the closely related white stonecrop. Yet another alien is the Indian balsam, a tall fleshy plant with showy pink flowers. Despite only having been part of our flora for a short time it has already gained two nicknames, including policeman's helmet, from the shape of its flowers, and jumping jack from the way its seed capsules explode when they are ripe, sending its seeds flying in all directions.

In spring, when the warm rays of the sun tempt us into taking a walk by the river, a strange little stuttering apology for a song draws attention to the male reed bunting. Clad in warm browns and greys, his striking all-black head and white half-collar makes him a dandy of the riverside, and we can forgive him his pathetic attempts at a song. He perches on the topmost twig of a bush or a reed stem, warning off would-be rivals from his territory, and at the same time hoping to attract the attention of a dull-coloured female in search of a mate. The four or five glossy eggs, brownish in colour and boldly marked with blotches and scrawls of black and chocolate brown, are laid in a skilfully woven cup-shaped nest of grass and moss, cosily lined with finer grasses and hair which is hidden in dense vegetation. Depending on the availability of nesting sites, sometimes this is on the ground, in a low tussock or in hedgerow bushes. Having moulted, in winter the male reed bunting resembles the female.

Reed bunting

THE RIVER NENE

COW MEADOW TO WESTON FAVELL MILL VIA BARNES MEADOW AND THE NENE WASHLAND

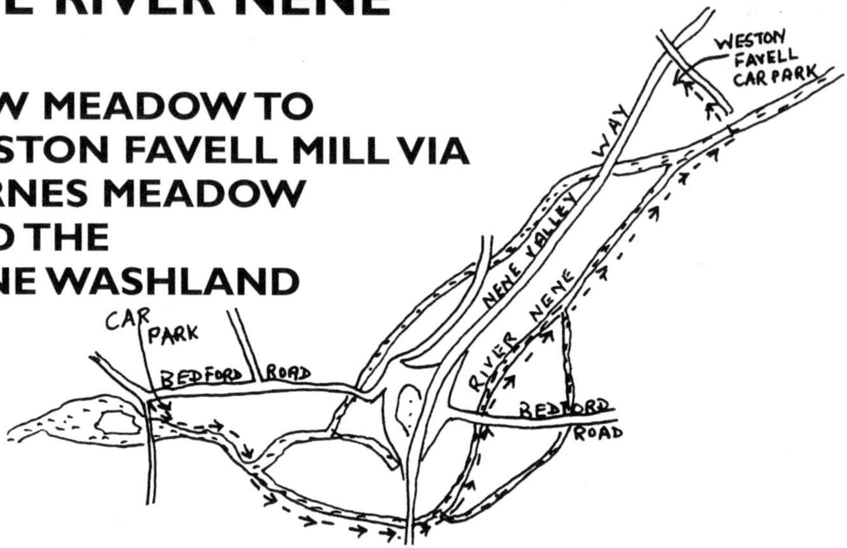

Another delightful walk is from Cow Meadow via Barnes's Meadow and the Nene Washlands to Weston Favell Mill. There is a car park off the Bedford Road close to the Cliftonville Road traffic lights. Or at the Weston Favell Mill end take the lane, signposted to the mill, and park on the far side of the bridge which carries the lane over the A45 dual carriageway.

Barnes Meadow Local Nature Reserve is a 28ha (70 acre) site which is managed by the Wildlife Trust for Northamptonshire, and situated on the southern edge of the town near the Barnes Meadow Interchange. Mainly grassland, it stretches from the Bedford Road back to Delapre Lake. It can be reached either from the car park in Midsummer Meadow or from the Barnes Meadow Interchange, where there is a small pull in before the A428 which leads into Northampton.

The area was 'created' when the River Nene was re-aligned some 25 years ago and it is now the redundant arm of the River. Now a very large 'pond', it is an ideal habitat for many forms of aquatic wildlife. Seventeen species of dragonfly and damselfly have been noted at the site, making it a very important area for these species. The grasslands are grazed by cattle, which keeps the sward low, and this benefits the flora found, which includes species like the ever-diminishing cowslip. The old railway track, a dry and sunny area, attracts a number of butterflies, including common blue, large skipper and red admiral. The marbled white has also been recorded in the reserve.

Golden Plover

The special bird of this area, and of the adjoining Clifford Hill gravel pits, has to be the golden plover. It occurs mainly from August through to March, its numbers building up spectacularly, to average over 3,500 individuals, and reaching a staggering 5,000 at peak times. This site now ranks as the eighth most important wintering area in the UK for this species, and is of international importance. From a distance the golden plover looks uniform warm brown above, and white below. In flight the massed birds show no special markings like wing bars or tail patches, but as they wheel and turn against a leaden winter sky they show first as indistinct dots, almost like smoke, and then flash clear white as they turn to show their undersides. It is vital that this important flock is disturbed as little as possible, so visit them by all means to see one of the nation's great wildlife spectacles, within the Borough, but please admire them from a distance

An uncommon wild flower, the flowering rush, manages to hang on close to the Cow Meadow car park, where a few plants may be found. There are others along the arm of the river to your left as you cross over the bridge. This misnamed plant is not a rush, but belongs to the lily family. A tall and stately plant it grows best with its roots in shallow water in quiet reaches of the river. It is nowhere common in Northamptonshire. The flowering rush is well worth seeking out from June onwards when its 2.5 cms wide clear pink flowers appear in large clusters at the tip of a bare and leafless stem.

Flowering rush

As you stroll along the river bank at this time of year, when there has been a spell of warm weather, you may hear the noisy splashes of large carp, as they excitedly thrash about in the weedy shallows during spawning. At times a huge broad brown-scaled back, with long dorsal fin, will be thrust clear of the water. After mating a mature female is capable of laying a million or more eggs. These are shed into the weeds where, given the right conditions, they hatch after only a few days. The tiny hatchlings - fry - become mature after five years, if they can survive the uncountable hazards which may face them during this period.

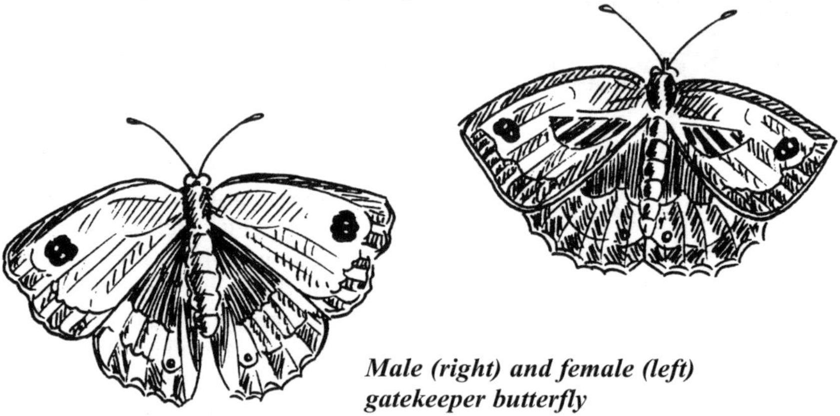

Male (right) and female (left) gatekeeper butterfly

The areas of rough grassland and scrub here are home to a variety of creatures according to the season. Prominent among them are the butterflies, especially those whose caterpillars feed on the tall grasses. They include Britain's commonest species, which is not the cabbage white as gardeners may think, but the meadow brown. At first glance it is dull brown colour, but the female has a large tawny-orange blotch on each forewing. You may see this if you can get close enough to it as it feasts eagerly on the nectar from the thistles. It is closely related to the gatekeeper, attractively named by the 18th century enthusiasts who watched it flitting to and fro between gaps in the hedges, and between gateposts. Smaller and darker than the meadow brown, a close view will enable you to distinguish male from female. If the butterfly has a clear tawny-brown patch on each forewing it is female, whereas the male has a dull black oblique stripe crossing the same area, as the illustration shows. The black marking is made up of especially perfumed scales, called androconia, calculated to drive

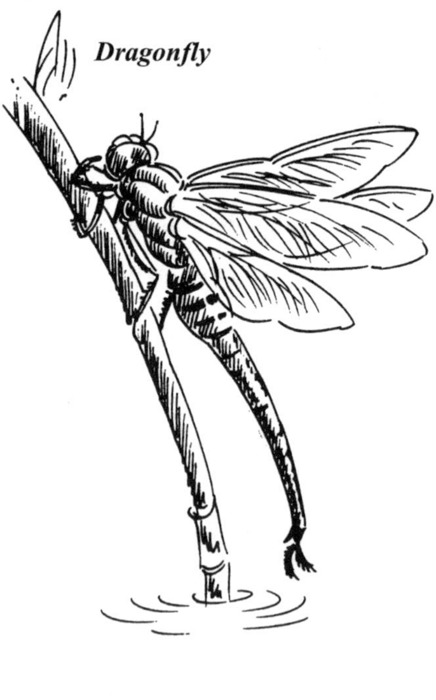

Dragonfly

the female wild with passion! Butterflies are well equipped to find their food plants; they smell through their feet!

This waterside area is also good for dragonflies and damselflies. Both groups belong to the same insect family. The generally larger dragonflies fly rapidly and rest with the wings held out horizontally from the body. Damselflies have a weaker-looking hesitant flight and hold the wings vertically above the body when settled. Half a dozen or more species may be found between May and the first of the autumn frosts, which kill off any stragglers. These airborne predators eat vast numbers of insects. The big hawker and darter species swoop to and fro, every now and then slipping sideways to snatch prey from the air. Small creatures, like greenfly, are eaten in flight, but larger prey, such as a daddy-longlegs, may be taken to a convenient perch to be consumed.

In the smaller species this adult stage occupies only a small part of their life-cycle, often no more than a couple of weeks. Larger species may survive for five weeks or more. The predatory larva, called a nymph, spends all its time under water, which may be as long as five years in some cases. When it is full-grown it crawls through the surface film of the water, and takes a firm grip of a reed-stem or similar secure perch. Then the skin across the thorax (the back) splits and the adult dragonfly or damselfly emerges. At first it is dull-coloured. The spectacular colours only develop after it has been able to feed for several days.

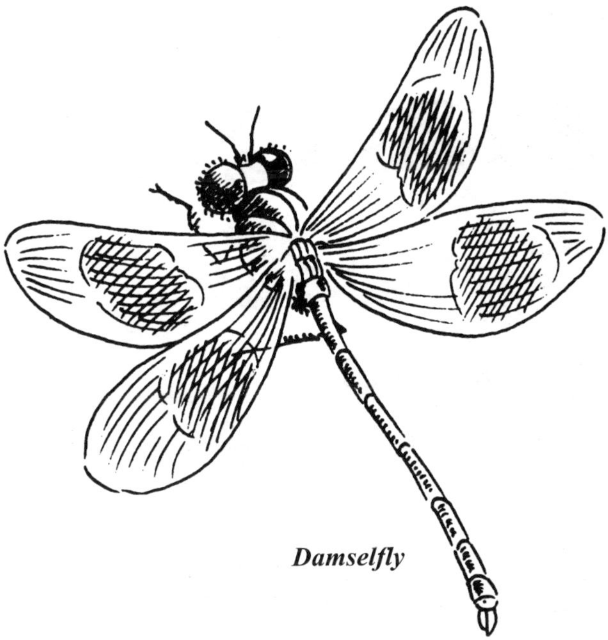

Damselfly

The expanse of rough grassland which leads up to the A45 road and beyond is the winter home of an uncommon bird which, half a century ago, used to breed in Northamptonshire. This is the stonechat which, as a breeding species, is now largely confined to the western districts of Britain, especially the coasts. The national population may amount to no more than 20,000 pairs. Although the stonechat often perches at the tip of dead plants, like thistles and docks, it is by no means an easy bird to find. It also dislikes too much human intrusion into its territory. A good way to look for it, between October and March, is to stand on the bridge and scan the area carefully with binoculars. It may be necessary to wait until it moves, when its darting, dipping flight, between one perch and another is distinctive. Its name comes from the alarm call which sounds just like two pebbles being struck together.

The area of the Nene Washlands, to the east of the Barnes Meadow roundabout and flyover, is excellent for wetland birds. These include many species of ducks and waders, and a telescope or good pair of binoculars is helpful in identifying them. Several species of gulls gather to roost here on bleak winter afternoons, having spent the day foraging in the town, or in arable fields maybe some distance from their communal roosting sites. Sometimes herons may be found standing around in the surrounding short grassland. I have seen as many as thirty which from a distance looked like so many little grey-clad hunchbacks. Approach them and they shoot out their long necks in alarm, before flying off in lumbering flight, on broad, square, long-fingered wings.

Roosting Starlings

AROUND THE TOWN CENTRE

Take a stroll from the town centre, along The Drapery and into George Row, where you will find All Saints' Church.

Rosebay willow herb

As you make your way to this historic building, instead of looking at the shops, follow the roof line, and you will soon discover plants growing there, fifty feet above street level. Most are the alien buddleia, introduced from China towards the end of the last century. This strange name was given to its family by Linnaeus, the great Swedish naturalist, in memory of Rev. Adam Buddle, a Lincolnshire clergyman, who lived from 1660 to 1715. He wrote an English Flora in 1708, and was highly respected for his botanical knowledge. The other scientific name for the plant, davidii, commemorates the great French naturalist missionary Father Armand David. The plant is also called *butterfly bush*, because from summer through to autumn its flowers are often loaded with butterflies, which come in search of its rich nectar supplies.

Another rooftop plant is the rosebay willowherb, with long narrow leaves, and a spike of flowers of deepest carmine pink. The books accuse it of being a plant of wayside and woodland, yet here we see it thrusting its roots into the masonry high up on a wall.

Its colourful flowers attract nectar seeking bees even here. But how do these plants come to be here? The answer is blowing on the wind. Both have small, very light seeds, those of the buddleia having tiny wings. The seeds of rosebay are each equipped with a cluster of long silky hairs, a miniature parachute which can carry them for long distances. As its seed pods ripen they dry out, and come under loose spiral tension. And then on a warm sunny day they spin open to set free their precious seeds to waft away on the slightest breeze. Its drifting seeds are among the first to colonise derelict land. Its flowers filled the bomb sites of London with a mass of colour after the first and second world wars, hence the alternative name of *fireweed*.

Even the elder bush finds a place among the rooftop plants. If it is allowed to grow on it will eventually cause structural damage to the building. But its seeds are far too heavy to drift on the wind, and they enlist birds to help them. The juicy berries are eaten by starlings and thrushes, and the seeds pass through their digestive systems unharmed. In fact they germinate better for having passed through the body of a bird. The seeds are ejected with other undigested food remains, so each is deposited with its own little package of *manure* to give it a start.

Stand on the steps of the church and listen. The best time to do this is early in the morning in spring or summer, before the roar of the traffic gets too loud. To the right a jostling head-bobbing knot of feral or street pigeons are picking at the scraps and the crumbs that have fallen from the delivery van that has just dropped off its cargo of bread and cakes at the confectioner's shop. Scurrying between them are urchin sparrows, and a few starlings, eager to take their share of the bonanza while it lasts. From a tree in the churchyard the simple, wistful phrases of a mistle thrush drift down.

If I were asked to name my top five bird songsters this bird would appear in it. Its song has a little of the quality of the blackbird, but nothing of the song thrush, each phrase made up of a few notes, seeming somehow hesitant. Sometimes it seems as if it is singing quietly to itself; at others it is surprisingly powerful. The blackbird may often be heard here giving the opportunity to compare their songs. Is it any wonder that it has been called the 'Mozart of the bird world'? There certainly is some justification for it. On many occasions, I have followed the development of the blackbird's song through the seasons, and listened to the bird polishing phrases, putting in a little trill here, leaving out a phrase there composing its song or so it seems to my ear. If you have a good musical ear, which I do not, you may hear fifteen song phrases, each one different from the others, before a particular phrase is repeated.

The monotonous calls of collared doves, another member of the pigeon family, are sure to be heard, to bring you back to earth with a bump. It seems odd to recall that until the mid 1950's this bird was unknown in this part of the world. Originally from India it has spread across thousands of miles of Asia and Europe, faster than house sparrows and starlings spread when they were introduced to North America. In 1955 they bred in Norfolk. Now their persistent ''ku-koo-ku" and moaning calls may be heard the year around in the town centre. The nest, a flimsy flat platform, is built in the

Collared dove

churchyard trees of All Saints. As vegetarians perhaps they, too, gather at the daily distribution of crumbs from the baker's vans, although I have never seen them compete with the street pigeons.

To complete a trio of pigeons, the wood pigeon also lives here. Larger than the other two it is mainly grey, but with a white half collar around the neck, and broad white shoulder flashes which are prominent when it flies. A close view in bright light will reveal the rich wine red of the breast, making it a handsome bird indeed. Its almost lazy crooning song sounds like 'take two coos, taffy take.'

Even rare birds occasionally turn up in this seemingly unpromising area. Three times I have encountered the black redstart, a summer visitor related to the robin, which has a national population of around 80 to 120 territory holding males. It is a specialist that likes derelict sites or large industrial complexes. In 1967, during the planning upheaval that tore out the heart of the town, a pair came to nest and rear their young where a brick had been dislodged from the wall of the old 'Chronicle and Echo' building, at the top of the Market Square, where Littlewoods is now. Ten years later I heard one singing its shrill, scratchy apology for a song, high up on a building, barely audible above the hubbub of market day. And finally, in 1983, one paused briefly to rest, and to sing a few song phrases, perched on the angelic wings of Saint Michael, above the Guildhall.

On a cold January afternoon, the street pigeons and sparrows will still be here, but on the Market Square you may be lucky enough to see a little black, white and grey bird running swiftly between the stalls, pausing now and then to pump its long tail vigorously up and down. The pied wagtail comes into town for the winter to eke out a living there. Its traditional roost site is in the dried up canes of a riverside reedbed, but the modern bird is not content with that. Increasingly it seeks the warmth of man made sites, like the canopy of the railway station in Kettering, or the loading dock of the Carlsberg brewery a few hundred yards from here, where up to 300 have been found.

Black-headed gull

Overhead the black headed gulls will be patrolling up and down, ever watchful for food scraps, and ready to rummage through discarded takeaway meal packaging for anything which will provide them with fuel to see them through the cold winter nights at their roost on the bleak Pitsford Water seven miles away. Their summertime home, perhaps in a freshwater marsh in European Russia, is but a distant memory as they square up to the problems of just staying alive. As the light begins to fade groups of them, numbering from two or three up to flocks of a couple of hundred, pass overhead. On a windy night they may battle along at just above rooftop level, but in settled weather they fly in typical V shaped formations.

These are the birds that have spent their day in the farmer's fields or at the local rubbish tips. But the town centre is itself the roosting site for a sizeable flock of other birds. Look up at the cupola of All Saints, late in the afternoon any time between November and March, and you will see starlings gathering there. They fly in, singly or in tightly packed flocks, to sit there, sometimes silently, at others murmuring amongst themselves as if talking over the events of the day. Every now and then a group of them takes off to fly around in tightly packed formation, turning as one, as if on a command, before returning to resume their perches. Soon there are several hundreds sitting there, silently, black specks against the verdigris of the copper dome. And then the whole flock takes off to wheel around against the darkening sky for one last time, before dropping down rapidly to their roost in the conifers in the churchyard. Hidden, they keep up their continuous chatter as they settle down for the night.

The town centre area is not all bricks and mortar. The churchyard of Saint Giles' has trees and seating, and plenty of wildlife to enjoy. Go through the Jeyes Jitty, the small opening directly opposite the entrance to All Saints, in the Drapery, turn right at the end and then left into Saint Katherine's Street, and you come to a small green oasis, where the church of Saint Katherine once stood. Here too, is a pleasant place to sit, with a variety of birds like sparrows and robins, and even the occasional grey squirrel with which to share your sandwiches.

LOOKING AT WALLS

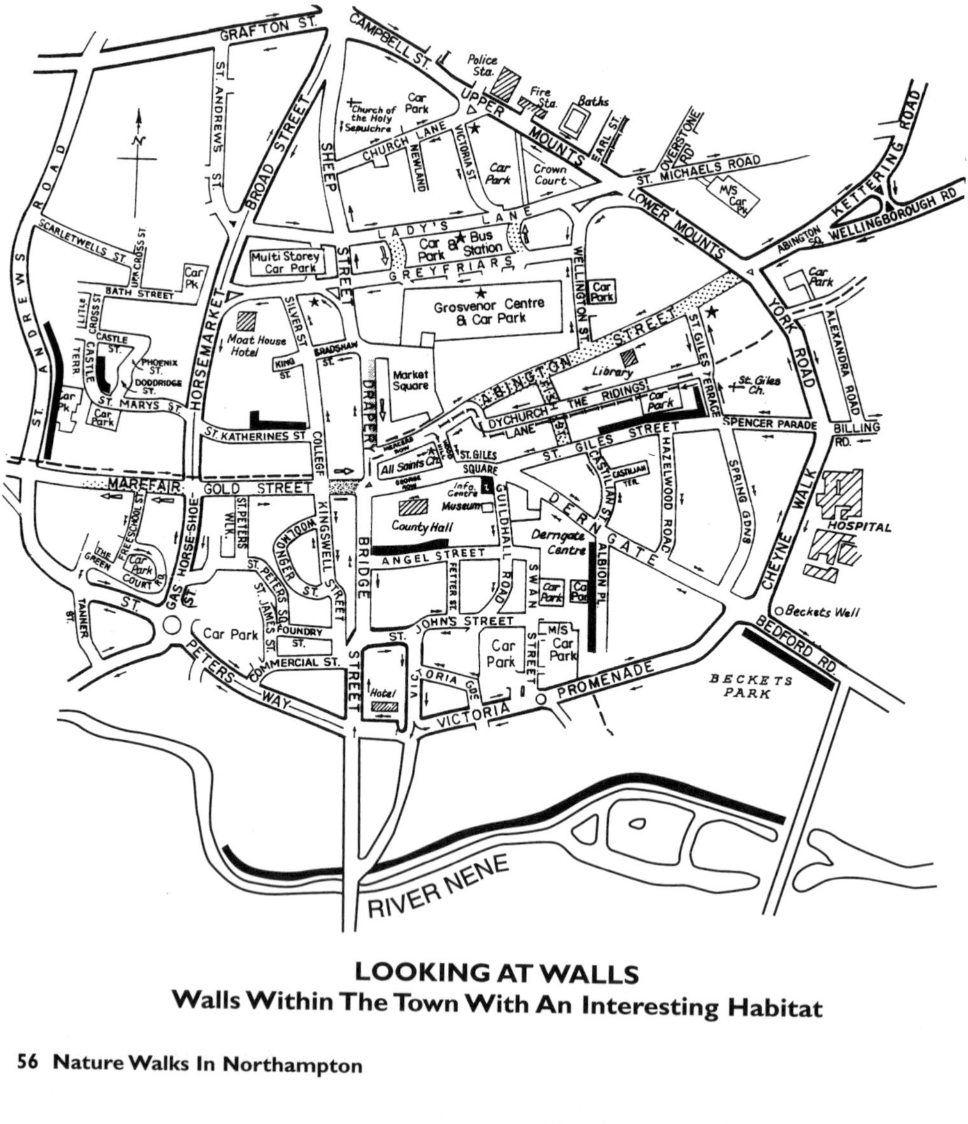

LOOKING AT WALLS
Walls Within The Town With An Interesting Habitat

Old walls can be found in various parts of the town, and especially interesting ones are highlighted and marked on the map, (page 56). Each is distinctive and will exhibit its own fauna and flora.

Nature is an opportunist and, as we have already seen, there are numerous areas which plants and animals can occupy in Northampton. In addition to large areas, like Abington Park and Lings Wood, there are also other apparently less hospitable places where wildlife finds a niche. Such areas include walls, rubble, the spaces around lamp-post bases, and street signs, as well as areas close to walls - in fact anywhere where seeds can germinate, and where animals can find a nook or cranny. For some species soil is necessary, and this generally arrives courtesy of the wind or people. Dust can be carried considerable distances: people can also carry soil - and sometimes the seeds of plants - from one place to another on their footwear and, in the case of seeds, on their clothing.

Even within a relatively small area there will be a diversity of walls and the materials from which they are built. A closer look soon reveals that some walls are more 'productive' for wild plants than others. Many are confined to specific areas of the wall. Newer walls need to weather to become 'established', before they support any wild plants. The weathering process is ongoing, and it is generally many years before a wall will be suitable as a habitat for wild plants. Add to this the fact that nowadays buildings, which are in use, are generally well maintained, and it often makes it difficult for plants to become established in these areas.

So, it is difficult to say how soon after construction a wall will attract its first plants, because whatever the building material a certain amount of weathering has to take place before anything 'settles in'.

With older buildings, such as churches, the exterior fabric is often more difficult to maintain, and such walls are more likely to provide suitable habitats for plants. So, churches, together with older boundary walls, tend to provide a better hunting ground for the plant enthusiast than newer ones.

Walls have different areas - zones - which are colonised by plants. The tops and bottoms of walls are most likely to provide suitable areas, with the top of the wall generally supporting the highest number of plants. A number of species become established either between the capping stones or on ledges. These include valerian, wallflower and stonecrop, together with other woody plants.

In addition to the top of the wall, it is also the base which is often a haven for a wide variety of plants. Here soil accumulates to provide relatively fertile material for many species.

Apart from the top and bottom of the wall, there are two other zones. These are only rough divisions and cover the areas from top to about half way down, and from this point to the base of the wall.

The building blocks are not the major factor to determine which plants arrive. It may seem strange, for example, that a granite wall supports lime-loving plants. This is because the majority of plants establish themselves in the mortar used for holding the blocks together. Having said that, there are some species which, although they may be found on any wall, favour certain characteristics. Stonecrop is more likely to be found where there is some acid. Hawkweeds - yellow composite flowers related to the dandelion - seem to appear more frequently in the niches on limestone walls.

The lower plants, like mosses and lichens, are less likely to be affected by the acid or alkaline nature of the wall, but more by the chemical composition and texture. Initially they need a surface to which they can become attached. Walls built from a variety of materials attract many of these lower plants, and different species are attracted to different areas on the same wall.

Within Northampton town centre people have been building walls for centuries, and although we don't have any which are as old as Hadrian's Wall or the Great Wall of China, some, are 'ancient'. And one of the oldest walls must be the wall built from stones which came from Northampton Castle, marking part of the boundary of the Northampton railway station car park, which used to be called Castle Station.

Many parks and gardens have old stone or brick walls. Before Northampton expanded, these features were also probably used to keep in cattle, to prevent them from straying onto adjacent land.

How porous walls are, and the amount of moisture they can soak up and retain, varies according to the material. The type of material also dictates the rate at which decomposition takes place, although other factors like exposure, amount of rainfall, and so on also have to be taken into consideration.

Examination of walls usually shows that the earliest breakdown of materials occurs in the mortar joints. Until the middle of the last century, walls were quite 'attractive' to plants once the decay process had started, because the mortar was made from lime, sand, loam, ash, straw and even dung. These materials had been used since medieval times, and it was only around the middle of the last century that a much harder mortar was produced, which included cement and pulverised furnace slag. With these harder materials the rate of decomposition is much slower. When older walls are repaired, the harder mortar is used. Although this change probably goes unnoticed by most people, it has meant that once-common wall species, like the moss *Encalypta vulgaris* and lichens, including species *of Lempholemma*, together with *Solorina spongiosa* and *Rhizocarpon concentriccum* have become much rarer because of these changes. Naturalists estimate that, on average, it takes between 40-80 years for certain parts of walls to be suitable for plants to colonise.

Not surprisingly, some of the most interesting plants occur on older walls, like those around some of the churchyards, and the remnants of the castle wall already mentioned, although during renovation of the latter, modern harder mortar was probably used. The aspect of a wall also has a bearing on the plants which will be found.

The most common wall plants in town are the lichens, many of which only have Latin names. Most are often overlooked. These lowly plants are slow growing, the rate varying from 1 mm to 10 mm a year. Crustose lichens - those patches which often look like stains - grow in all sorts of places. Although they prefer limestone, they also grow on concrete, cement, mortar and, where they still occur, on asbestos roofs. The commonest of these lichens is the greyish-white *Lecanora dispersa*. Where there are large patches - like those found on church and churchyard walls and old gravestones - it is an indication that they have been there for a very long time.

Because they are so common, and many are, to some extent 'nondescript', they are seldom given a second glance. But you are less likely to overlook *Xanthoria parietina*, one of the foliose lichens, and *X. aureola*, a related species. Both of these can still be found, but are less common than they used to be. They grow on walls, roofs and occasionally trees, and are noticeable because they are either an orange or deep yellow colour. Where these particular species occur, it is a sign that the air is clean. Lichens are used as pollution indicators, and when the number of pollutants in the air increased due to industrialisation, these plants were poisoned, and many disappeared from former areas. Fortunately in many places - including Northampton - the air is now much cleaner, and some lichens are returning, although they take many years to grow into larger patches to reach their former size.

The other group of widespread wall plants is the mosses. Again, like the lichens they are taken for granted. But look at a moss plant with a magnifying glass and it becomes much more interesting. Different species have different shaped leaves, and they also harbour a number of very small creatures which take refuge and shelter amongst the tightly packed cushions of leaves. By comparing lichens and mosses immediate differences can be seen. Lichens do not have distinct stems and leaves: moss plants do. It is not unusual to find two or more moss species growing in the same area, so that the plants intermingle, making identification difficult, although few species grow on walls. As with other wall plants, mosses are often confined to certain areas of the wall, and

Silvery thread moss

like lichens, these are some of the first plants to come in. They are useful because, once they start to grow, they trap water, making the wall moist, which helps with the breakdown of the mortar. As mosses die and decay, they provide minute traces of minerals and humus, which can be used by other plants.

One of the more common species is silvery thread moss, which grows in cracks between the bricks and stones in walls. This moss has very closely woven silver leaves, which trap blown dust, increasing the area where the moss can grow. Where quite large amounts of dust accumulate, the silvery thread moss may spread quite quickly. A closer look at the plant shows that the upper parts of the leaves are green, due to the presence of chlorophyll. As with all green plants, it is these leaves which, with energy from the sun, and minerals from the wall, can make food.

Wall screw moss

All mosses produce capsules which contain spores, which are almost the equivalent of seeds of flowering plants. New plants may grow from these. In addition to the production of spores, silvery thread moss has another means of spreading. The tips of the leaves are brittle, and easily break off. When it rains, water runs down the wall carrying these away, and if they find a suitable site they may start to grow.

Another common town moss is the wall screw moss, which is found on wall tops, and forms small, neat-looking closely-knit silvery tufts, which are around 2-3 cm in diameter. In dry weather this moss doesn't die, but instead goes into a 'resting stage' during which the leaves change colour, 'screw up' and turn greyish - hence its name. When it rains the moss starts to grow again.

Maidenhair spleenwort

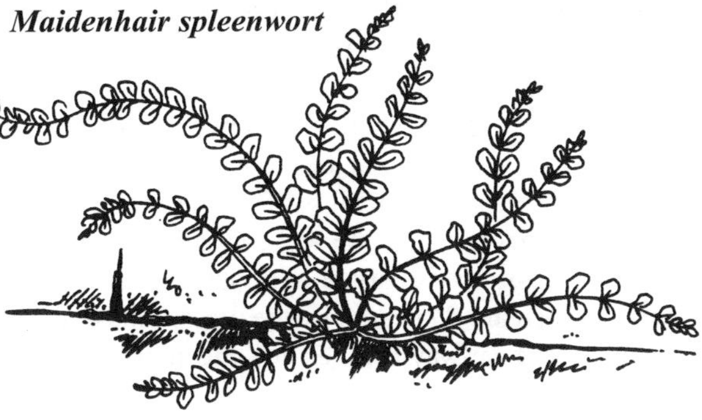

Not unlike the wall screw moss, matted thread moss is found in similar places on the wall, but the ends of the leaves do not have the silver colour.

The ferns, another group of non-flowering plants, also occur on walls. In the days before walls, the ferns, now referred to as 'wall' ferns, were confined to rocks and boulders, growing in amongst crevices where trapped soil had collected. It is easy to see how they have transferred to walls, which provide similar niches. There are generally many cracks and crevices in older walls, as well as on the tops of walls, not to mention the roughened surfaces of stones and bricks. Here soil becomes trapped, to provide the initial material for the wall-living ferns. Most ferns need a chalky or limey surface, and they occur where there is mortar between bricks and stones, Old walls provide the largest number of places for ferns.

Wall rue spleenwort

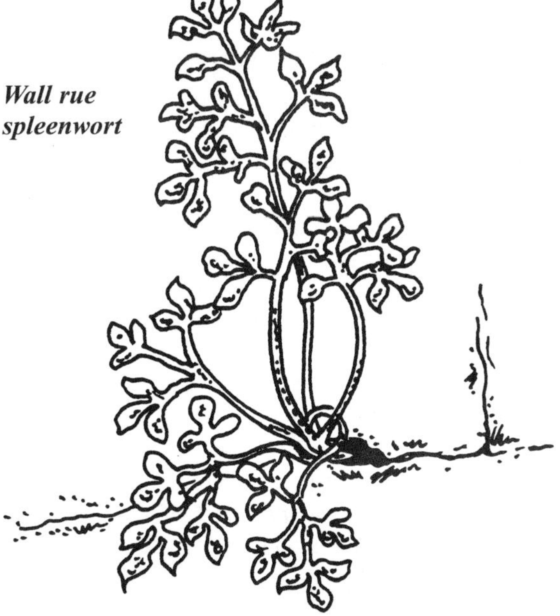

As with many other places, towns are less hospitable than they used to be, and fewer ferns are found now than about a hundred years ago. Maidenhair spleenwort is one of the most common town ferns, and because of its wide distribution it has the alternative name of 'common wall spleenwort'. Unlike the mosses and lichens, this is a much more noticeable species, with its deep green sprays of 'leaves', which in the case of the ferns, are known as pinnae - pinnule singular. The plant brightens up old walls where it grows, and in Northampton you can find it under the railway bridge at West Bridge. At certain times of the year, the spores develop on the back of the pinnae, and once these are dispersed they may be transported to suitable places in which to grow.

One wall fern, the wall rue spleenwort, got its name from a flowering plant. Its leaflets - pinnae - are similar to the leaflets of the meadow rue, and although the fern grows in other places, the wall is often the habitat which it favours. The stems grow up from a short rhizome, and the leaves, with a leathery surface, twist in dry conditions, an adaptation possibly evolved to conserve water. The plants produce a large number of spores, which are dispersed by the wind. This one too grows at West Bridge, and also on the mortar of railway bridges at Kingsthorpe.

The books suggest that the harts-tongue fern occurs in mixed woodland, but it also grows on a number of brick walls in Northampton, and can be seen at several sites, including basement walls in the town centre, where it has colonised areas between the brick, in the mortar. Here it obtains some of the basic nutrients, and provided there is a continuous supply of moisture it will thrive. This is different to all other species of fern, because the leaves are not divided. The wall does not provide the same level of nutrients as does woodland where it is also found. This is reflected in the much smaller size of the strap-like leaves, sometimes only 2 or 3 centimetres long.

One wall-loving species, pellitory of the wall, is a member of the nettle family. It has an interesting adaptation for living here. Once it becomes established in a suitable crack or cranny, it sends out a number of roots, which penetrate into other cracks between bricks and stones. Closer examination reveals that the stems are distinctly reddish-brown, and the stalked, glossy leaves, grow alternately along the stems. In June clusters of tiny greenish-brown flowers appear: these are extremely interesting because there is a distinct difference between the stamens and stigmas. Female flowers have reddish-brown feathery stigmas: in the male flowers the stamens are especially conspicuous because of their yellow colour. These stamens, set in boat-shaped sepals, have a fascinating way of shedding their pollen. When the pollen is ripe the sepals reflex, arching up the filament - the stalk which carries the pollen-bearing stamen - and this puts it under considerable pressure. Either an insect crawling over the plant, or a strong wind, will cause the filament to spring upright. When this happens the pollen is ejected, and shoots off.

It is not surprising that when early botanists studied this method of pollen release they dubbed the pellitory of the wall the ‘artillery plant’. When the oily seeds are ripe ants collect them for food. Although some reach their destination, many will be dropped en route, and provided conditions are suitable, pellitory of the wall will colonise new areas. Pellitory-of-the-wall is found in the stone walls of the Doddridge Memorial Chapel.

Ivy-leaved toadflax

Another fascinating wall plant is the ivy-leaved toadflax. Not a native of Britain, it was introduced from southern Europe in the seventeenth century to be grown in gardens. Like many other alien species it wasn't long before it 'escaped', and once free it rapidly colonised walls in various parts of Britain. Now quite widespread, where it becomes established it quickly covers large areas of the wall. An interesting plant it has long trailing stems, which are smothered in small leaves, and when in bloom it sports attractive purple and yellow flowers. Each two-lipped flower has a rather long nectary, containing the sweet-tasting liquid, and the plant will be at its most effective for propagation, when the stigma is ready to receive the pollen, and the plant 'turns' it away from the wall. Bees searching for the nectar, also pick up and carry the pollen. Once pollination has taken place, changes start to occur. The seed capsules which develop are held on long thin stalks to reach the light. When ripe it points towards dark cracks where the seeds will eventually be shed. Here, hopefully, some will germinate to give rise to new plants. White flowered varieties occur at Kingsthorpe.

Several species of *stonecrop* may occur on walls, and because of their weak roots, they often prefer well-lit and exposed sites which are near the tops of walls. Although they produce flowers and seeds, many stonecrops grow by the fragmentation method, where small pieces of leaves fall off, and start to grow in other places, including the base of walls.

The *biting stonecrop* is widely distributed, and the plant occurs in a variety of habitats, from walls to the roofs of older houses. It has adapted its lifestyle to cope with

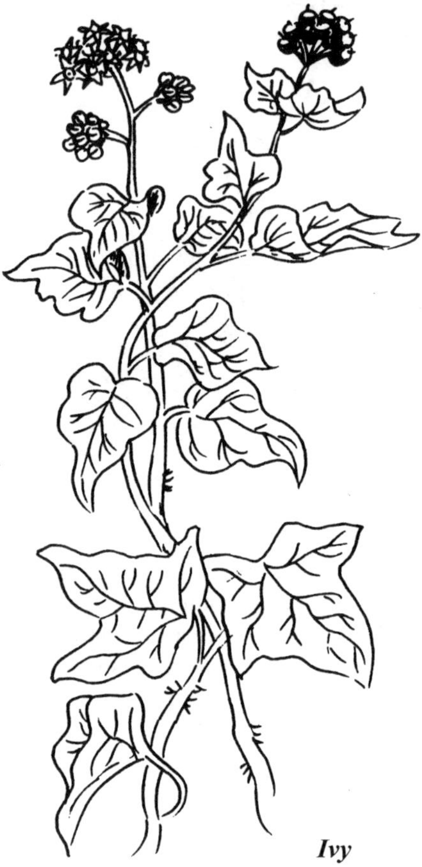

Ivy

difficult conditions, when water becomes scarce or non-existent. Its fleshy leaves have evolved to conserve this precious liquid, and once it becomes established, it seems to thrive on drier walls, where it survives even in drought conditions. Its alternative name of *wall pepper*, comes from the slight peppery taste of the succulent leaves. When the star-shaped yellow flowers appear they almost smother the plant. Both this, and the white species, are common on the site of the old gasworks.

Ivy is another plant which makes use of the wall - but for support rather than for food. It is usually rooted in the soil at the base of north or east facing walls. Ivy plants germinate from seeds usually dropped by a 'careless' bird! If allowed to grow unattended, ivy forms such 'dense' patches, that it prevents other plants from gaining a roothold! Although it does not damage masonry with its roots, its sheer weight may have a disastrous effect on some older buildings, perhaps leading to their collapse.

Ivy plants have two types of leaves. Those which are deeply lobed (segmented) grow on the vegetative branches, especially where they use their adventitious roots to climb up the wall. The others, either heart- or spear-shaped, are found on shorter stems which bear the flowers and then the fruits.

From the suction pads many smaller - adventitious - roots grow, but these only hold onto the wall, and do not penetrate into the cracks. Yet, if a cutting is taken, and pegged down on soil, these same roots will grow.

Coming into bloom later in the year, the first flowers usually appear in September; the last in November. These flowers are small and greenish-yellow in colour, and are arranged in globular heads. They produce an abundant supply of nectar, which provides a source of nourishment for late insects when most other supplies have dried up. Flies and wasps are especially attracted to the sweet-tasting liquid, and their visits are important because they are responsible for pollination. Once fertilised, the flowers fade, and the berries start to grow. At first they are small, green, and inconspicuous, but gradually change colour until they turn black, exhibiting a ribbed surface. Because these seed-carrying berries appear later in winter, they provide nourishment for birds when other food is scarce.

One plant which should be found on walls is the aptly named *wallflower*. Not a native, it was introduced from the eastern Mediterranean, and is now widespread in Britain. Where it is grown as a cultivated species it is a biannual - not producing flowers and seeds until its second season. On the wall the plant becomes more 'constricted', and unlike the garden variety it does not generally die back after its second year, but remains in situ, effectively making it a perennial. When compared to the cultivated species its flowers are much smaller. Mortar-rich soils on wall tops are one of its favourite places, especially where there are sunny aspects, although it is not particularly tolerant of pollution from sulphur dioxide. The wild wallflower produces bright yellow-orange flowers, and like pellitory of the wall, once the seeds are ripe, ants carry them off.

Another wall-loving species, the first flowers of which originally exhibited a showy burst of dark red flowers is the *red valerian*. Now the blooms are generally mauve-pink, or occasionally white, possibly because it is a different species. Like the wallflower it is not native, but was introduced during the Middle Ages from the Mediterranean where it grows on limestone cliffs. After pollination, the seeds are equipped with parachutes which assist them to disperse. Unlike most wall-living plants, this is one of the few to cause damage to stonework.

Some plants, more familiar in other habitats, may be found on the wall. These include members of the compositae - those with composite flowers. Several species of *hawkweeds*, have become colonisers, where they are often found on the tops of walls.

The *dandelion*, related to the hawkweeds, and a familiar member of the compositae, is often found on walls. The well equipped seeds, with their parachute dispersal mechanism, are carried long distances, and provided there are suitable niches will start to germinate in cracks in walls, as well as at the base, where soil accumulates. Once established, they can live for considerable periods.

There are a number of grasses which may become temporary wall residents, but one in particular, the wall barley, is usually found. It wouldn't be right to look at the wall, without mentioning many other species, although they may be short-term residents. These include chickweed, shepherds purse, red deadnettle, goosegrass, and sow thistle.

ANIMALS OF WALLS

Springtale

If most wall plants are conspicuous because of their foliage and flowers, it is necessary to search a little harder for wall animals. Because of the protective nature of the wall, together with many damp areas, the wall is an important refuge for many different species: others come because there are suitable places for webs or for making nests. Although the wall may be suitable for much of the year, in hot weather, it can become so difficult that one naturalist likened it to an arid desert. Richard Jefferies, that perceptive 19 century naturalist, spent some time looking at walls, and in his book *Open Air*, he particularly referred to these areas, noting that, *'Every crevice is the home of insects or used by them for the deposit of their eggs - under the tiles or slates, where mortar has dropped out between the cracks...'*, and he continued ...*'Sometimes a sparrow may be seen clinging to the bare walls of the 'house'. Tits do the same thing. It is surprising how they manage to hold on. They are taking insects from the apertures of the mortar. Where the slates slope to the south, the sunshine soon heats them, and passing butterflies alight on the warm surface, and spread out their wings, as if hovering over the heat. Flies are attracted in crowds sometimes to heated slates and tiles, and wasps will occasionally pause there'.*

Some of the smaller insects, including the primitive springtails, find suitable homes in the wall. The springtail species found in a particular wall varies, and it is difficult to generalise. Some come to feed on the plants, including the lichens. Others need nothing more than dead and decaying vegetation for nourishment, and the wall provides them with a supply, especially where plants like ivy, have became established.

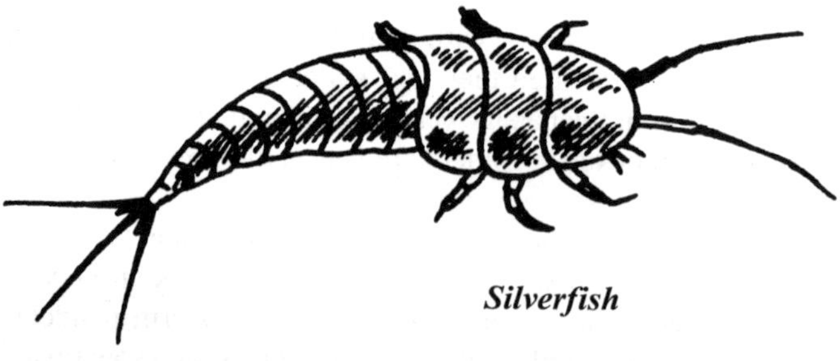

Silverfish

The most primitive insects, are also attracted to walls. 'Ancient' wingless *silverfish* have a long lineage, and belong to the group known as bristletails. They are covered with extremely small silvery scales, hence *silver* and *fish* in the name. They need shelter, and where ivy festoons the wall, these small insects may be found.

Ivy, and other spreading plants, also provide shelter for woodlice, the common garden slater often being the most likely species to be discovered. Woodlice are crustaceans and their relatives - the crabs and lobsters - still live in the sea. These small invertebrates - animals without backbones - need a moist atmosphere if they are to survive. Intriguing creatures as you can discover in the chapter on producing your own wildlife garden (page 76), one other species which makes its home between loose mortar of brick walls is the pill woodlouse - the species which 'curls' up into a ball, and which was swallowed by our ancestors because it looked like a pill! Although in need of moisture, it seems able to tolerate the drying out of its habitat, although in extreme conditions it will move off to seek 'pastures new', where the moisture content is higher.

Niches in walls also provide several species of *snails* with a home, including the *garden, banded* and *white lipped* species The presence of these molluscs is often given away by the slime trails which they leave when they go off on their nightly feeding sorties. Debris in and around the wall provides them with enough sustenance, but they may occasionally venture further afield, and it is worth taking a careful look at old walls in particular to discover where they have been 'roving'.

Many walls support the *garden snail*, which is fond of sheltered crevices at the base, especially between bricks and mortar which have been eroded. Overhanging coping stones at the top of walls often provide a suitable shelter for the garden and other snail species. If the weather becomes too warm snails avoid drying out by going into a temporary state of 'hibernation', known as *aestivation*. When this happens the opening to the shell is sealed with mucus, protecting the otherwise vulnerable creature inside. Sometimes groups of garden snails become cemented together by their epiphragms - the disc used to close the opening to the shell.

Walls provide innumerable cracks and crannies for *spiders*, including web-spinning species, like the more dramatic orb-web building *garden spider* as well as other common species.

Those webs referred to as 'cobwebs' can hardly be overlooked. The word 'cob' means a 'flimsy structure'. The webs of these spiders are especially untidy, and seem to be put anywhere, whether in the corner of a garage or old cellar - anywhere where there is enough support, which many walls provide. The same species may take to the outside window sill, where there is some protection, for the spider if not for the web. It is true that older, darker houses, especially along passageways and alleyways, attract this particular species. But the spider is not too fussy, and loosely bonded stone walls are particularly favoured, where the creature may produce extremely fascinating - even spectacular - tubular nets.

These web-producing spiders include *Ciniflo*, known as the sieve and comb spider. The webs of this animal can usually be found in almost every crack and cranny - and in walls of any age. They will use modern brick walls, as well as older ones. Unlike the superb orb-webs of the garden spiders, those made by *Ciniflo* are particularly 'untidy', the creature appearing incapable of producing an attractive structure. Having a white or blue-white tinge, with a lace-like pattern, they are slung across to cover any convenient cracks. Once constructed, the spider takes to a hiding place, The centre part of the web often looks dirtier and untidier than the rest of the structure. Hidden during the day, *Ciniflo* emerges on its food-hunting expeditions at nightfall. The sticky silk provides an effective trap for all sorts of creatures, and from late summer through the autumn, the legs of dismembered insects, and especially craneflies, may be seen. These webs are worth investigating regularly for the 'bits and pieces' of a variety of insects left by the creature.

But by far the most 'spectacular' and intricate webs are those made by the orb-web spinners. The spiders produce these almost anywhere, and a couple of autumns ago, I opened the curtains to discover an intricate structure which had been suspended from the corner of the window to the lower frame. This remained for many days, and was repaired and renovated as necessary on a day-to-day basis. The female was often spotted early in the morning, carrying out her renovatory duties. There are several species of orb web makers, including the familiar garden cross spider, with its distinctive cross on its back, and *Araneus umbraticus*, which unlike its relatives is a night-time hunter. The spider usually seeks a nook or cranny where it can hide, but we recently had one inside a building in town, which was clearly visible throughout the day, although it remained close to the roof of a porch. 'Disturbances' to the strands of the webs to tempt it from its 'lair' proved unsuccessful. It is worth taking time out to look at these webs, which are 'works of art'. Certain threads have droplets of glue on them, and it is this sticky fluid which helps to trap the spider's prey, and alerts the spider via a signal thread leading to the lair.

Not all spiders make webs, and there are many other wall-living or visiting species - which never bother with this type of 'trap'. But, as with all spiders, they are capable of spinning silk. Various species of *wolf* and *zebra* spiders will find the wall a suitable place to live and find food. Wolf spiders are aptly named, using the technique practised by the mammal of the same name to catch its food. Initially using a stalking technique they pursue their prey, eventually pouncing on it, injecting a poison, and sucking out the body fluids.

Zebra spiders belong to the group known as jumping spiders. As their name suggests they have striped bodies, like their larger namesakes. This striped coloration is particularly effective on a wall, and these small spiders, measuring some 5-6 mm in length, are very difficult to detect. When observed, they practice an interesting means of surprising the prey. They 'sidle' up to it, and then with a sideways jump, take it by surprise. Always alert, the spider is helped by eight eyes, with the two front ones showing under a microscope's magnification as extremely large powerful headlamps. At least one species occurs on walls, especially during the warmer months of the year. Although the spider does not make a silken web, it pays out a silken thread before making a leap to ensure that, if it has an 'accident', it will have a lifeline which, should it miss its footing on a wall it will not crash to the ground!

We have already mentioned that ants are responsible for the dispersal of the seeds of at least two wall plants. *Ants* inhabit suitable sites in the wall, especially where there is loose mortar, and here they may construct small nests.

So far we have looked at animals which colonise walls without doing any particular damage, by taking advantage of the sites already provided. But some species which target the wall can cause considerable damage. These include the solitary bees and wasps. Not all walls are suitable, and although in general older ones are more vulnerable to 'attacks', we have lived in two relatively new houses, both of which have been targeted by these hole dwelling insects.

There are several species of *mason bees*, which as their name suggests, are 'masons', digging holes and laying eggs in the softer mortar. The problem with modern cavity wall houses, is that these insects can damage the insulation. The female either finds an old tunnel which she takes over, or excavates her own. The female is fairly easy to distinguish from the male: she has a short pair of 'horns' on her head. Once she is satisfied that it is ready to use, she treks off to collect damp soil which she mixes with saliva to form each cell. As each one is finished, she produce a suitable 'door'. Then she makes more journeys in search of pollen, which she takes back to the 'house'. A single egg is laid in each individual cell, where there is a supply of pollen to provide food for the larva once it emerges.

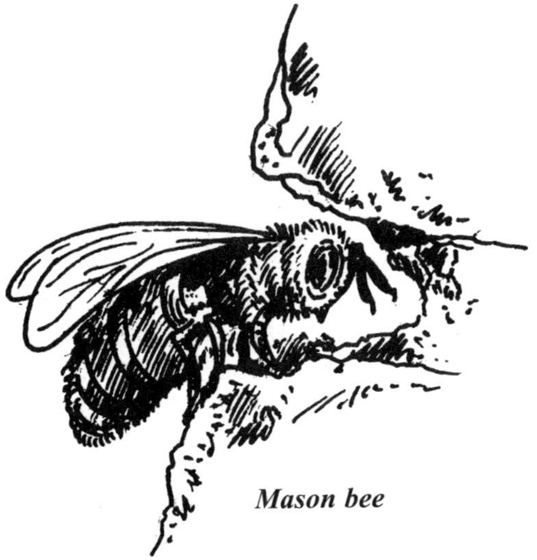

Mason bee

The mason bee is not safe in its retreat, because the ruby tail wasp may make an attack. A parasitic species, the female lay her eggs in the nest of a mason bee. Once the larvae hatch, not only do they consume the supply of food, but they also eat the occupants.

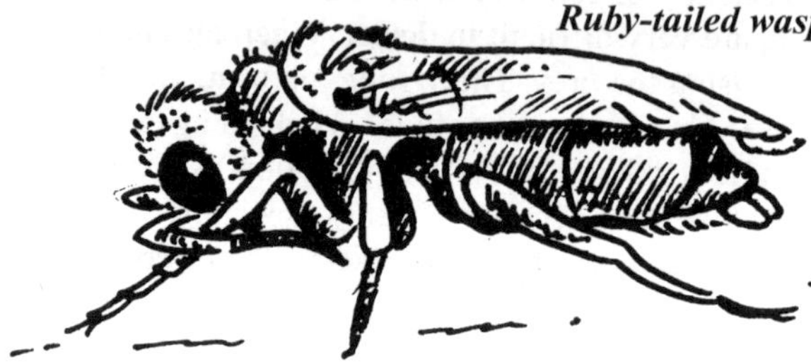

Ruby-tailed wasp

There are many other invertebrates - animals without backbones - which occur in the wall, especially where there is some vegetation cover. Centipedes, millipedes, earwigs, and on some occasions slugs, may all take up residence, much as they do behind the loose bark of trees. Other species, like the small tortoiseshell butterfly, may seek out places to hibernate during the winter, as will queen wasps. And even the caterpillar of the small white butterfly might find a suitable place to pupate and spend the winter, ready to emerge in the following spring.

Wren

Two birds which might find nesting holes in walls are the robin and the wren. Having chosen a site which may be a hole in a wall, the female robin makes a bulky cup-shaped nest using a mixture of grass, dead leaves and moss. The first robins lay their eggs in March, and the last probably in June. Between three and six eggs are laid, and the female incubates these for between 13 and 14 days. Most robins have two broods, and the very early nesters may manage a third.

Although the female is responsible for incubating the eggs, the male helps her feed the young, and together the parents bring a variety of insects for the nestlings. Feeding lasts for 12-14 days, when the young are ready to fledge and will leave.

The wren may also choose a hole in a wall, although, like the robin, this is only one of a variety of sites where the male may build a nest. In fact he seems to take a delight in nest-building, and produces several from which the female makes her choice. His well-produced nest is domed and made from moss and grass, but there is no lining: This is left for the female once she has chosen the one in which she will lay her eggs.

The first wrens nest in April, slightly later than robins, and there are up to ten eggs in each clutch. Like the robin, the female takes charge of incubation, but her mate assists her once the eggs hatch. Together they feed the growing offspring on a variety of insects.

POCKET PARKS

The unique concept of the pocket park originated in Northamptonshire, and six of these areas are within Northampton. Managed by local people, they vary from well-established sites to newly created habitats.

Blackthorn Pocket Park

is in Cherry Lodge Road, on the Eastern side of the Borough.

Grid Ref: SP808636.

This area is a newly created site which the residents have taken over. It is in the centre of a large housing estate, and was designated a public open space by Northampton Borough Council.

This once-open area has been transformed by local people. Hedges have been planted on two sides of the meadow. Native shrub species were used for this, not only as an attractive addition to the area, but also to provide a valuable habitat for wildlife.

In addition, local people have established a raised bed and, to provide access for wheelchairs, a pathway has been put in. To give an indication of the area and what is present, a board has been erected, which gives information about the site.

Boughton Lane Pocket Park

is on the Boughton Lane.
Take the Kettering Road North out of Northampton,
and at the first roundabout about a mile from the town centre,
take the exit to Moulton, along Moulton Way,
and into Boughton Lane.
In just over a quarter of a mile,
turn into the pocket park, and join the footpath
and turn right to follow it between the hedge.
If you have trouble locating the entrance,
the footpath is on the left where the houses run out.
If you have a car, park in Cottingham Drive
on the opposite side of the road.

Grid Ref: SP767655.

One of the most fascinating aspects of pocket parks is that no two are the same. At Boughton Lane Pocket Park, which is on the Boughton Lane, the group has acquired a site which is long and thin, measuring about a mile from one end to the other, and with a maximum width of about 200 metres. In effect this makes it a linear pocket park. An interesting feature is that it is flanked on either side by old well established mature hedges.

Originally Boughton Lane Pocket Park was a boundary site, variously known as the 'Deer Park', 'Northampton Park' and 'King's Park'. The land, which belongs to Northampton Borough Council, was acquired from the New Towns Commission. It is now managed for the local community by South Court Environmental.

A wall, which runs almost the complete length of the site, has an associated hedge. The former, which is built from local stone, has always caused problems and easily falls into disrepair. In the past it was the responsibility of the local parishes to maintain the structure.

Half of the length of the site has been designated a Site of Local Conservation Value.

Such a long site demands a great deal of maintenance. At present work on the Park is aimed at keeping the mile long footpath clear of brambles, which is almost a full time job. On the social front, two events annually attract a great deal of interest. In the summer there is a barbecue and on All Hallows Eve, Flight Night takes place. In the case of the latter, people arrive disguised by masks and carrying candles; sparklers are also hung in the trees to add to the atmosphere.

Great Billing Pocket Park

is off Penfold Lane next to the cricket ground.
It links the village of Great Billing and
the new settlement of Ecton Brook.
Grid Ref: SP812632.

At Great Billing the pocket park is a meadow where an extensive programme of tree planting has taken place around the perimeter. Like Blackthorn, it is also on the eastern edge of the town, and provides a green oasis amidst a large area of new housing. In addition to the planting scheme, a variety of habitats have been created, including a butterfly garden. An annual activity, which has become extremely popular is haymaking, so much so that not only does it involve members of Great Billing Pocket Park, but also other volunteer workers who come from far and wide to help out.

Levi Strauss Pocket Park

is in the grounds of the Levi Strauss factory
on Deer Park Road, off Redhouse Road/Talavera Way in
Moulton Park Industrial Estate.

Grid Ref: SP774648.

Apart from local communities, one of Northampton's well-known firms has become involved with the pocket park movement. Within the grounds of the Levi Strauss factory the employees have got together to ensure the survival of an old spinney. In addition to planting a new hedge and creating a wildflower meadow, the group has also put up nestboxes The work of those involved with the Levis Strauss Pocket Park was acknowledged when the firm was given a Northamptonshire Business Environmental Award for their initiative in setting up the pocket park.

Nettle Gap Spinney

Wootton is off the Newport Pagnell road.
Turn into Lady Hollows Drive, then second turning on left
into Thrupp Drive. The Pocket Park is on the right.

Grid Ref: SP772566.

Nettle Gap Spinney, on the edge of the new Wootton Fields housing estate, was neglected for many years before local residents decided to 'take it under their wing'.

With a clean up programme, linked to the planting of new trees - many of which have been raised from seed - and the erection of bird and bat boxes, the area has taken on a new lease of life. Access is being improved, and a stream which runs through the spinney is also being cleaned out. In future an adjacent meadow will form Phase 2 of this Pocket Park.

The Cloisters

Spring Boroughs is on Upper Cross Street, opposite the Spring Boroughs Community Centre.

Grid Ref: SP751607.

The Pocket Park was named after the area's historical associations with the medieval St Andrew's Monastery, which was a feature of the area many centuries ago. In addition, The Cloisters also has close connections with the history of the former Castle. In Spring Boroughs the local group responsible for the Park has drawn up a five year management plan to take care of the site. Activities include the planting of shrubs, climbing roses and a scented rose hedge, all of which have been put in to enhance the appeal of the area. These measures are also proving attractive to wildlife, and to improve this aspect of the site even further, bird and bat boxes have also been erected. A small wildflower meadow is also a feature, and there is a table with seats for those who want to have picnics. With new path layouts, rustic fencing and pergolas, the Pocket Park is a joy to the residents of this area of the town.

Spring Lane Lower School, renowned for their interest in the environment, also has links with the park. Work in school, where seeds are grown and compost made, is linked to regular visits to monitor and record the wildlife, making this an important addition to their school-based activities.

For more details of the Pocket Park initiative, contact Sue Paice, the Pocket Parks Officer. Details will be found under the 'How can I help' section on pages 92-94.

PLAYING YOUR PART

A vast array of wildlife which, through the centuries, once lived within what is now the Borough of Northampton has disappeared in relatively recent times. The increase in the human population of more than 56,000, from 133,670 in 1971 to 187,700 (estimate) in 1995 - a 42% rise - almost speaks for itself. As more and more land disappears it leaves fewer and fewer sites for wildlife. Although most people won't necessarily condone this, nevertheless they recognise that this is the price to pay for progress. But all is not lost: there are ways in which people can do their bit in a small way to help redress the balance. But most people will quite rightly say 'how? The answer, without question is in the back - or even front - garden.

At first sight such areas may not seem suitable for wildlife. But pause for a moment. Unless you are especially unfortunate bees visit your garden whether by choice or by accident. Butterflies probably flit in and out, even though you may not see them. And when you are tucked up in your bed, your patch may be visited by many species of moths - not to mention a variety of other animals. And during more hospitable times of the year the number of night-living insects which are likely to be on their rounds, paying you a call, may run into hundreds of different species. Even on a cold winter's evening your patch may attract its fair share of wildlife.

Hedgehog

And that's only a start! The size and position of your patch may entice a variety of feathered friends, and it is possible that the occasional mammal, such as fox, badger or even muntjac, may take advantage of your territory, deserting their haunts for yours. And for many urban dwellers the sight of those cigar-shaped black droppings around the garden - on both lawns and paths - are the 'calling cards' of that prickly garden visitor, the hedgehog, or as some folk call it, the 'urchin'.

For some people in town there is no back garden, and they may have to make do with a balcony: some won't even have this. But don't despair! What we are suggesting is that no matter what your plot is like you can do something for wildlife, and hopefully increase your invitations to a wider range of visitors, in addition to those which may already be around.

What is ideal for some wildlife may not be so for others. Even with a relatively large area you may still find that you have to cut your suit according to your cloth. But anyone can have a wildlife garden within even the smallest area.

Defining *'wildlife garden'* is relatively easy. It is an area which has been planned for wildlife. But that doesn't mean that an area ***not*** planned for wildlife won't attract it! Whatever size your patch you can use it for wildlife. There are various ways of doing this and the ideas in this section will help you. But because we don't have very much space here, you will need to consult other books.

Wildlife Pond

Before you do anything make a plan of your area. This will give you a good indication of what you have, and allow you to juggle around with your ideas before deciding what is best. Mark on any features which already exist - like ponds, trees, fences, etc. Some of these may already be encouraging wildlife: others may be useful for all sorts of reasons. If your garden is large enough you may be able to provide a number of different areas - habitats - for wildlife. These could be for aquatic animals or for birds - or both. If you have a smaller area try an instant garden. Having produced a plan the following information should help you decide which areas you can fit in.

Perhaps the term 'instant garden' is misleading, but it is more instant than some of the other ideas. In fact an instant 'garden' doesn't need a garden! It consists of a collection of containers which, if carefully planned and arranged, will attract wildlife. The advantage of this system is that a wide range of containers can be used - many of which can be purchased quite cheaply. You can use large plastic or terracotta pots, as well as tubs, wooden planters and old chimney pots - not forgetting to mention disused sinks or even baths. If you don't have room for these then choose a window box.

Containers with suitable plants attract a variety of insects. Apart from providing these small visitors with nourishment, you will also be able to watch a wide range of creatures from the almost 'top heavy' bumble bee to the more agile butterfly. If you include some night scented flowers, moths will come too including - in the right season - those large delightful hawk moths.

Plants can be grown from seed, bought from a nursery or purchased by mail order. Check flowering times to ensure you have a succession of nectar-producing flowers for as long as possible. Choose plants for sun and shade, selecting species which won't grow too big for your containers.

Planting tubs and containers is easy. Put small stones or pieces of broken pottery at the bottom to allow for drainage. Half fill with garden soil, or one of the peat free substitutes. Place your plants in your containers, leaving space for growth. Add more soil, and firm with your hands. Water in the plants, and then water daily in the evening once the sun is down. Use natural or recycled water. Once in flower, check regularly and dead-head, which - for many species - should encourage more flowers to grow. Keep seeds for germinating in the following spring.

Birds

With a little effort most gardens - from the smallest to the largest - can attract birds. In the past, winter and spring were seen as the times of the year when birds needed the most help - and it wasn't the 'done thing' to feed during the breeding season. But research carried out by the British Trust for Ornithology (BTO) has revealed that the most dangerous months for birds are March to July. These months can prove dangerous for many birds, with 'lean pickings' Feeding the correct food might save a lot of birds from starvation. It should also be remembered that prolonged cold spells during the winter is bad news for many birds.

As with humans, birds know what to, and how to, feed their young. The bird table and hanging basket are important at this time of the year. A regular supply of black sunflower seeds, in transparent feeders appeals to many seed-eaters. Blue and great tits, and greenfinches readily take them. Peanuts, placed in wire mesh feeders which have metal tops and bottoms (to prevent squirrel attacks), are also suitable. Birds can only take small pieces of nuts which won't choke any nestlings.

Bird table

Nest box on tree

Some birds, like the house sparrow, are in decline. These and other species need live food - like meal worms. Either breed your own, purchase from a local fishing tackle shops, or buy by mail order from firms like CJ WildBird Foods - who also stock wax-worms. The siting of summer feeding stations is important. Check for cats and squirrels, and move the feeders and bird table around to prevent the accumulation of harmless disease-carrying organisms. Provide water and dust baths which need to be kept topped up. Dustbin lids sunk into the ground are ideal.

During the winter and early spring almost any food can be given to garden visitors. Since bird feeding might become a full time hobby, consult the various books to provide you with all the information you need to make it successful. Never waste any leftovers. If it can't be given to the birds, put it in the compost bin! A bird table is a must! The handyman - or woman - can produce one from 'scraps of wood', but the less 'competent' might have to buy one. Choose one with a roof and with a rim around the table. Plastic is easier to keep clean, but wooden ones allow you to add a mesh cover to prevent the larger birds from lifting all the food! Always remove uneaten food regularly, otherwise it goes off - and birds can get food poisoning

If space is at a premium use a hanging bird table and suspend it from a wall or hang from a tree - taking the necessary precautions to deter predators.

If you would like your birds to become residents, try putting up bird boxes. Different birds have different needs, so consult a suitable book. Even in a small space, a patio wall will take a box. If it is occupied you will have enjoyment at close quarters. Don't forget that it is illegal to interfere with any breeding bird.

Get the position right, and ensure that the bird box will not be affected by prevailing cold winds, and that it is shaded from the sun. Bird boxes should face anywhere from north through to south east. Adults and the young birds must have a clear flight line in and out of the bird box.

Insects

There is nothing more indicative of a warm summer's day than to hear - and watch - bumble bees as they come in search of nectar. They will stay if there is a source of food. So, consider the bees - and don't forget the butterflies. Both groups of insects need nectar. Plan your planting so that you have a sequence of nectar-producing flowers from spring through to late autumn. This means you will also have a continuous parade of visiting insects. Some of your plants should be early-flowering, so that insects waking up from hibernation have food. They also need a supply of nectar before hibernating in the autumn. Where space is at a premium, plant up containers, window boxes, or put a butterfly bush - buddleia - in a tub. Plants suitable for butterflies and bees usually attract moths, but include some night-scented plants for these nocturnal insects. Where possible choose south or south west facing sites, and 'butterfly' plants should be out of the wind in a sunny area.

Annuals need replacing every year, so save on costs by planting perennials. Initially more expensive, they are better value for money in the long term. Where you have a border 'grade' it with tall flowers at the back and shorter ones at the front. *Gardening for Wildlife by Ron Wilson, published by Capall Bann*, lists suitable plants. Collect seeds from as many plants as possible and hand some to friends to enhance their gardens for wildlife.

Mammals

It is much more difficult to plan a garden for mammals, since they are even more 'elusive' than birds. Some species, like rats, shrews, mice and maybe voles, probably visit some gardens regularly. One other, the grey squirrel, is not always welcome. But its antics can be quite entertaining, and provided the bird table is protected all should be well.

A frequent visitor to many gardens, including those in towns, is the hedgehog. With an ever diminishing countryside, gardens become more important for wildlife, and it may be one of the few places which provides hedgehogs with food. Urchins - as some folks call them - are useful pest controllers, and a good reason for encouraging them to the garden. Provide food for hedgehogs from late summer to early autumn - they find their own for much of the year. Leave tinned cat or dog food outside in a saucer each evening, and keep your eyes open for any visitors. Don't give milk, because it upsets the hedgehog's digestive system. If hedgehogs visit your garden they may stay for the winter! In autumn they produce an hibernaculum - a winter sleeping nest. This is little more than a 'duvet' of dried leaves, which protects and insulates the mammal from the worst of the cold weather. To make the hedgehog even more comfortable provide it with a 'house'. A simple hedgehog house can be made from an untreated wooden box, with a 4 to 5 inches square (10 to 12.5 cms) hole cut in one side. Big enough for hedgehogs, it is too small for cats, dogs and foxes. An entrance 'hall' can be made from bricks. Cover the whole with polythene, and then coat with leaves and brushwood for camouflage and extra insulation.

Foxes visit many urban gardens, and if you have them, regular feeding will encourage them to call most nights. Muntjac, or barking deer, are now also found in many areas in town. About dog size and some 46 cms at the shoulder they feed from dusk until dawn. They need relatively little cover. Frequent sitings of the mammal are made in Northampton.

The badger - brock - is now turning up more often on urban patches. Increasing demands on the countryside have made the badger a virtual prisoner in some urban environments. Discover whether there are setts in your area, and if there are keep an eye out for badgers in your garden. If they come, feed with sultanas, raisins, peanuts, maize, etc. If you have a lawn they may find a supply of earthworms - their favourite food.

Badger

Bats visit many town gardens. Insect-attracting plants also attract bats. Putting up bat boxes may also encourage them to roost - or even hibernate. They are protected mammals, and must not be interfered with. If you suspect a bat has taken up residence in a bat box, carefully lift the lid so that you can investigate. Once discovered the bat must be left alone. If you want to continue to investigate then you must obtain permission from English Nature (01733 340345). If they take up residence in, for example, you loft and you need to carry out work there, you must seek advice from English Nature.

Pipistrelle

Wild Areas

Have a wild area in your garden to encourage wildlife. This will be 'weedy' and may provide hiding places for small mammals, an area where insects can shelter, as well as providing a supply of nectar from any flowering plants. Introduce a large patch of stinging nettles if they don't occur naturally. Common butterflies, including peacock, small tortoiseshell, comma, and the migratory red admiral, all lay their eggs on these plants. To prevent them taking over the garden, plant nettles in containers, or place a sunken fence around them. Locate nettles in winter and bring them to your patch. Keep the shoots cut back to about 3 to 4 inches (7-10 cms).

Leave piles of leaves and other garden debris in the garden in autumn, because it could provide hedgehogs with a winter home. Put in piles of stones and/or bricks for a range of invertebrates - creepy crawlies. A piece of corrugated iron, or similar corrugated material, makes a useful hiding place for a range of invertebrates, not to mention some small mammals.

Leave upturned earthenware plant pots, and some sacking or old carpet (not foam-backed) around. As the sacking and carpet becomes damp it provides a useful habitat for a variety of invertebrates. A pile of dead wood is also valuable, because as it decays it provides a multi-storey habitat for wildlife - a bit like a large housing estate. In a well-established pile there could be as many as a thousand different species of invertebrates.

Water

Water is vital for wildlife, and providing a permanent supply - apart from bird baths - is valuable. If you can't put in a pond, adapt other utensils. Old sinks and baths are useful and should be sunk into the ground. Sinks also make interesting above-surface water features when placed on brick walls. Most water areas generally 'stock' themselves.

If you want to put in a pond, consult a suitable book - and make it as attractive for wildlife as possible. In cold weather icing over can be a problem. When ice forms put a small container on the surface and add hot water. Repeat until it makes a hole in the ice. This allows harmful gasses, which might build up, to escape. Don't break the ice: it could injure fish. Keep a block of wood or ball in the water which will usually leave a hole.

Composting

We are all continually being encouraged to recycle, and many of us do this with bottles, tins and newspapers. Recycling household and garden rubbish is also important, not only because it means fewer land fill sites, but also because it is a cheap way of producing compost for the garden. Everyone has household waste, and even with a small garden, there is also some waste from this source. Other items of household waste, which may not usually be considered suitable for composting, including old pure woollen jumpers and sweaters, can be put into the compost bin.

Plastic bins are suitable, and tried and tested bins include the Rotol Compost Converter, recommended by the HDRA (address on page 93). Alternatively, make wooden bins, which should be covered with wire mesh, and lined with an old piece of carpet. Other home-made compost bins can be constructed from a series of one metre square frames made from 5 cm square timber. Stack them on soil to allow liquid to drain away. Cover with a wooden lid or old carpet.

Composting is a versatile way of getting rid of a lot of waste, but it isn't a way of disposing of ***all*** household rubbish. These do's and don'ts will help. Don't use newspapers (recycle them), ash from fires/solid fuel boilers, or glass, plastic, and metals (recycle). None of these turn into compost. Use some autumn leaves, but if you have an excess recycle them by putting them in a separate bin or heap. Scraps such as meat and fish should ***not*** be used, although other kitchen waste, such as egg shells, teabags, peelings, vegetable remains, etc. are okay. Disposable nappies are not suitable. What you put in has different composting times.

You can safely add items from the vegetable patch, and bedding from small mammals, like gerbils and rabbits - but not cats. Garden weeds, dead flowers and old flower plants are suitable, as are hedge clippings, like hawthorn and privet. Chop up the stems as these take longer to compost.

Some farmyard or horse manure with straw helps to add bulk to your heap. Other items, such as grass clippings, and chicken manure speed up the composting process. Add these, and plenty of compost material and it may raise the temperature of the compost to between 55 and 70 degrees centigrade. Some heaps never get hot. This isn't a problem: it just takes longer for the material to decompose. If the heap dries out, add water. If it gets too wet, add some bulky dry material.

Turn the compost from time to time, by taking it out and mixing it up, to speed the decay process. Compost develops first at the bottom of the bin, so check these layers. When ready, sprinkle around the base of plants.

YOUR GARDEN NATURE RESERVE

There are plenty of books about some garden visitors and inhabitants. like birds and mammals. This selective section covers some of the smaller creatures which make up the garden 'nature reserve'. We realise that some Northamptonians are luckier than others. What we hope to do is to 'whet' your appetite so that you will discover just what an interesting place the garden often is. You will find much more information about the wildlife garden nature reserve in 'Gardening for Wildlife' by Ron Wilson, published by Capall Bann.

Stone habitats

Woodlouse

Stones - whether placed singly or as a rockery, harbour several species of wildlife. Woodlice - piggies some people call them - live here as well as under plant pots, bricks, the wheelie bin - and anywhere where it is damp and dark. Crevices in bark, and damp leaves in hedges, also provide suitable haunts. Woodlice are Crustaceans, and many people are surprised to discover that they are related to crabs and lobsters. Useful in the garden, they are ideal refuse collectors - devouring some of the rubbish we don't need. The lifestyle of these seemingly uninteresting creatures is fascinating. Of the 42 recorded British species, 29 are native. Those which can roll into a ball were used in herbal medicine. People suffering from digestive problems were given woodlice to swallow!

Although a land lubber when compared to its relatives, it has not totally shed its aquatic habits. Although hard, the skin is not totally waterproof, and if woodlice stay in the open for long periods they dry up and die. That is why woodlouse often - literally - hot foot it, across paths or patios on very warm days. Its hiding place has probably become too hot for comfort, and it is searching for a cooler and potentially safer spot.

To survive and breathe the bodies of most woodlice need to be covered by a thin layer of moisture, through which gasses are exchanged. However, when totally immersed in water they drown. In the breeding season the female develops a brood pouch under her body. During the breeding season overlapping plates on the underside of the body grow to form a carrying structure. When growth is complete these plates literally form a false floor to the female's body, and the pouch fills with liquid. The female lays her eggs here. It probably takes about a month for the eggs to develop into woodlice, when the fluid drains away very vulnerable woodlice are left. One expert described them as being 'no larger than grains of rice'. Within a few days the pale-coloured young leave the pouch, and a few days later, shed their skins. They continue to grow until they are replicas of the adults. Because woodlice have hard exo-skeletons, growth can only take by shedding the skin. When this happens they seek shelter, and half white and half black woodlice may be encountered in a hiding places.

Silk Spinners

Mention the word 'spider', and most people almost literally run for cover. No one is certain why these creatures have such an effect on most people It has been suggested that it is because of the speed at which they move. But do try to stop long enough to discover more about them.

Not all spiders make webs, although these are the ones which are most noticeable. One of the most spectacular of the web-spinners is the garden or orb web spider - from the orb-like design of its web. Pull the blinds one autumn morning, and you may have a visitor, as I did. There on the outside corner of the frame was the most exquisite web. Liberally sprinkled with dew, the early morning sun added an extra dimension. The web was there for around ten days. In the evening it was often ragged, the threads damaged by marauding insects. In the morning it was repaired: sometimes the female was there carrying out her chores. After some ten days the web became more tattered. There was no sign of the female. Her mission was accomplished, she had mated and gone off to lay her eggs.

Like many other garden creatures, spiders are friends rather than foes. Carnivores, they catch and kill other small creatures. The method used for catching food varies, but once 'trapped' poisonous venom is injected through curved needle-like fangs. Some venom is lethal enough for a quick kill, whereas other poison merely serves to paralyse the catch. In spite of the production of poison, no British spider is dangerous.

Although a few species may 'attack' the skin; if poison is injected it produces no more irritation than a nettle sting!

By far the most enterprising activity is the production of silk. All spiders produce this, and although not all use it for web-making, every species uses silk for wrapping around their eggs. Silk is produced in glands in the abdomen and released through spinnerets, each of which is made up of a number of extremely small nozzles. The silk is pulled out from the spinnerets, and the hind legs are generally used for this. You can see this happening when the spiders are either wrapping food or making and repairing webs. When web-making, spiders either move or even swing away, and the silk is drawn out behind here. Once secured to a suitable object, web-making progresses in a structured way. Silken threads are also used as safety lines. You may have seen small spiders swinging from ceilings on their silken threads. Similarly spiders use this method of escape if they are under threat.

Each spider can produce three or four types of silk. In female spiders a special silk is produced and used for protecting the eggs. The egg cocoons vary: many are yellow in colour, and pushed into cracks and crevices for protection. Some spiders roll their eggs in soil to camouflage them. Others, like female wolf spider, keep their cocoons 'strapped' securely to the abdomen.

Many insect-eating spiders spend the winter as eggs, and in the spring when up to 300 spiderlings emerge from a single cocoon they may be seen on walls or fences. Such large numbers are unlikely to find food where they emerge, and each minute spiderling take a chance and launches itself on a silken thread, so that the wind will carry it to new areas and food.

Spider numbers are phenomenal. W. S. Bristowe estimated that an English meadow may have as many as 2 million spiders to the acre, although there are probably fewer on your lawn!

Beneficial bees

I find nothing more soothing and relaxing than to watch an over-laden bumble bee moving from flower to flower in search of nectar. All bees, together with butterflies, hoverflies, and wasps, bring about pollination. But a recent disturbing report shows that hundreds of these essential insects are in decline. The most important groups of pollinators are the bees and stinging wasps. Of the 495 species, nearly half - around 200 - continue to decrease in numbers - and 18 have already disappeared.

Bumble bees are in trouble due to the destruction of habitats and use of pesticides. Comparing the present day with Victorian times it shows that not only are the insects in decline, but so are many of the plants which they relied on for pollen and nectar.

What is particularly worrying is that not only will many of our garden flowers and vegetables remain unfertilised, but so will crops like oil seed rape and beans. This means that seeds, for which they were planted, may never be produced.

Your garden tomatoes rely on the bumble bee, and scientists have discovered that the high pitched buzz of the insect 'encourages' the tomato to shed its pollen. Because of the serious decline of these insects it has been necessary to import foreign bees to do the job.

Other small inhabitants

Other invertebrates to keep an eye out for include the ladybirds (there are many species) and lacewings as they prey upon the aphids - blackfly and greenfly - on your beans and roses. What efficient pest controllers!

Centipede

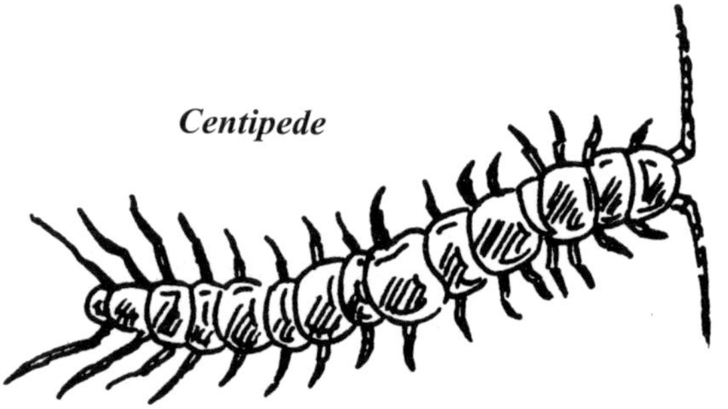

Centipedes and millipedes may be discovered amongst the vegetation. Centipedes need moist areas, and damp leaf litter is often a suitable habitat. The collection of debris at the bottom of a hedge is a good place to investigate. Other centipedes live in the soil. These predators come out at night to feed. Armed with poison fangs they capture their prey and inject lethal liquid into their victims.

Millipedes are often confused with centipedes. Apart from differences in leg arrangement - centipedes have one pair of legs per body segment: millipedes have two - the bodies of centipedes are always flattened: millipedes are round. Because they catch and kill live food, centipedes generally move more quickly than millipedes, which have a more 'leisurely' attitude to life! Young centipedes can grow new legs: older centipedes aren't able to do this, but still remain mobile. Forty four different species of centipedes are found in Great Britain, some of which arrived on alien plants. These foreigners have found a niche - although many have moved only short distances from the point of arrival.

Of the soil-living centipedes those most often seen are the long and relatively slender types - the geophilids - which means 'ground lovers'. Living in the soil, eyesight is superfluous, and these centipedes produce a phosphoflourescent liquid, which protects them by making them visible, so frightening off any would-be enemies. When disturbed some members of this group produce and give off a distinctive almond aroma. In spring each female lays between 30 and 40 eggs in the soil, and she then coils her body around them for several weeks until they hatch. If the eggs are left they go mouldy, and it is thought that she licks them regularly to either get rid of or prevent mould from developing. She remains with her young until they are independent.

Other centipedes seek refuge under logs and stones. These are the shiny brown ones which dash off when they are exposed. Having a different lifestyle, they belong to the group known as lithobiids - the 'stone-dwellers', and have longer legs enabling them to attain a reasonable turn of speed, necessary when capturing food or escaping from would-be enemies. Only two of the seventeen species of lithobiids are commonly found in gardens. One, known as *Lithobius forficatus*, is a deep chestnut brown, and varies in size from 18 to 30 cms. This is the one which literally 'legs it' when you disturb it under logs and stones - not to mention seed trays and plant pots. If you have a compost heap (see page 83) then these centipedes are in their element feeding on any creatures which might also seek refuge here.

Like centipedes, millipedes also seek out damp, dark areas, and stones, logs, seed trays and flower pots - as well as the compost heap - usually harbour them. Although some species are harmless in the garden, others are classed as pests. Most millipedes are long, slender animals, and those which spend their lives in the ground have no eyes. Although some millipedes may climb trees, especially in damp weather, the majority live on the ground, searching in amongst leaf litter and the soil for their food. Some species of millipedes may be abroad during the day, but most are active nocturnally, and like centipedes and woodlice they are found where there is some moisture, otherwise they dry up and die. Some species are useful because they help break down plant material, speeding up the decay process. Others live in the nests of ants, and here they are thought to act as refuse collectors, consuming bits of debris left over after the ants have fed.

But not all millipedes are friends of the gardener. At least one species - the snake millipede - can prove disastrous, because it feeds on roots and other crop parts. The snake millipede is especially active during very dry conditions when researchers think they are in need of moisture. Once damaged it is likely that the plant tissues will continue to be attacked by the millipede. To protect itself, the creature produces what is in effect a repellent. Foul- smelling and tasting, these fluids are meant to deter would-be enemies, but they are only partially successful. Amphibians, birds, small animals, together with some species of spiders feed on them.

Millipede

Pill millipedes roll their bodies into balls and this is another way of effecting protection. When picked up by prey, these coiled millipedes are much more difficult to swallow than the elongated ones.

Butterflies and Moths

Of the larger invertebrate visitors to the garden, the butterflies, and to a lesser extent some moths, are particularly noticeable. Several species of butterflies may be seen, and if you have a supply of nectar (see page 80) then you may attract them, and if nettles feature in your wild area (see page 82), then breeding butterflies may be a feature of your patch. Nectar-imbibing species, like the small tortoiseshell, peacock, and the migrating red admiral, are likely to be the most noticeable. Depending on where you live, you may also have painted ladies, the notorious whites - small, large, and to a lesser extent perhaps green veined - and the early emergent brimstone may pay you a call. Various browns - hedge (or gatekeeper), wall and ringlet - may make appearances. Of the moths the most spectacular are species of hawk moth which turn up from

Garden tiger moth (right) and the woolly bear larva of the tiger moth.

time to time. These include the eyed, hummingbird, poplar and elephant - a mere fraction of more than two thousand different species of moths which are found in the British Isles. A number of these may be garden residents. Because of their nocturnal habits, the majority of moths go about their business unknown and unseen by humans. We tend to notice them when they are attracted to lights.

One of the other distinctive garden visiting moths is the garden tiger, a delightful insect with contrasting chocolate, white and orange wings. It might seem strange that the moth should want to advertise its presence, but the bright colouring and a distinctively unpleasant taste act as warnings to would-be predators to stay clear! I am distasteful, the moth declares!

With only limited space to explore the garden nature reserve, we hope we might have whetted your appetite to get out to explore your own patch.

HOW CAN I HELP?

There are many ways in which you can help, and these ideas are not exhaustive. Pay a visit to your local main library, look on the notice board, access Genie, and take a look at the Environmental Contacts list produced by Northamptonshire County Council.

British Trust for Conservation Volunteers, The, (BTCV) is a national group with a Northamptonshire branch. It organises work parties to carry out conservation work. Some tasks take place in the Borough: others around the county. Contact the Organiser, Moulton College Moulton, Northampton, NN3 7RR Tel: 01604 643653.

Brockwatch and North Northants Badgers. The groups encourage members to check on setts, report dead badger sitings, interference with setts, etc. Both groups monitor and report on setts where various development in an area is to take place. Details of membership - and how you can help - from Steven Jackson, 01327 706349 or Eddie Parsons, 01536 760141 (Brock Watch/Northants Badgers).

Butterfly Conservation. A local group of the national organisation is based in the county. It encourages people to take an interest in butterflies. It also carries out conservation and research. Details from either John Elliot (01933 66392) or Nigel Muddiman (01604 758909).

DITO (Drop in the Ocean), South Count Environmental. *01604 630719.* This is a project aimed at encouraging people to make, at least part of, their garden environmentally friendly. For more information about the services available contact the above number.

Friends of the Earth has a local group with the national aims of informing and empowering the public, and is involved in local, as well as national, campaigns. For more information contact 01604 639583.

Gardening for Wildlife - *Sources of Information and Supplies* covers suppliers, organisations, books, etc on birds, butterflies, hedges, mammals, ponds, trees and wildflowers. £1.25 (includes postage (from Ron Wilson, Darby House, Welton, Daventry, NN11 5EJ.

***HDRA (Henry Doubleday Research Association), National Centre for Organic Gardening**, Ryton-on-Dunsmore, Coventry, CV8 3LG.* The leading European organic gardening organisation. Produces a wide range of leaflets, seeds, compost, etc. Comprehensive catalogues available.

Nene Valley Project is run by Northamptonshire County Council with support from national and local bodies. The Project has responsibility for the whole of the Nene Valley, including the area within the Borough of Northampton. For further information contact Cheryl Joyce on 01604 237227.

Northamptonshire Bat Group aims to carry out research, and keep records of the distribution of bats. It welcomes sightings, and details of injured bats. Contact Phil Richardson on 01604 770632.

Northamptonshire Bird Club organises meetings, bird watching sessions, etc. Details 01604 880009.

Northamptonshire Environmental Forum has been set up as part of the Local Agenda 21 initiative, and a number of Topic groups have been meeting regularly. These cover Pollution, Energy, Community and Awareness, Traffic and Transport, Social Wellbeing, Countryside Recreation and Development and the Economy. For further details contact 01604 236738.

Northamptonshire Fox Welfare Group consists of people interested in the welfare of these often maligned mammals. For further details contact Martin Hemmington. Tel 01933 411996.

Northamptonshire Natural History Society is based at the Humfrey Rooms, Castilian Terrace in Northampton. Various groups meet regularly with indoor and outdoor meetings. There are 'specialist' groups for walks, microscopy, meteorology, astronomy, etc. Details from 01604 604529.

Northamptonshire Women's Environmental Network aims to educate, empower and inform women who care about the environment. It arranges meetings and seminars. For details of the local group contact 01604 810647.

***Parish Paths Project Officer, Environment Directorate**, Northamptonshire County Council, P O Box 221, John Dryden House, 8-10 The Lakes, Northampton, NN4 7DE.* Able to offer advice about parish paths. Contact 01604 236236.

***Pocket Parks**,* Northamptonshire was the pioneer for these areas. There are a number in town, including those at Blackthorn, Spring Boroughs, Boughton Lane and

Levi Strauss. Each park 'belongs' to the people and is managed by them. If there is an area of land close to you which you think would make a suitable pocket park, contact Sue Paice, the Pocket Parks Officer on 01604 237222, and ask her for help and advice.

RSPB *(Northampton group).* Local group has regular meetings and activities. Welcomes all levels of expertise. John Dunn 01604 505607.

Rotol, Original Organics, *Units 4/5, Farthings Lodge Business Centre, Plymtree, Devon, EX15 2JY.*
Manufacturers of the Rotol compost converters, and made from 100% recycled plastic.

South Court Environmental is made up of workers who form a co-operative and has twin aims:

(1) Supports wildlife conservation and ecological work for the benefit of communities and
(2) Supports communities in benefiting wildlife conservation.

Members of the group have various skills, which are employed in the above

in practical conservation
in wildlife survey work
in ecological research
in research methodology and computing related to the environment
in fund-raising for the community and wildlife
in networking and publishing.

They operate STORE, which has a number of strands, including the buying and selling of books from members/member groups, it supports nature conservation in Northamptonshire, and helps support overseas communities working in co-operative self-reliance. For more details contact 01604 630719 or 01604 250856.

Tree and Lansdcape Officer, Environment Directorate, *Northamptonshire County Council, P O Box 221, John Dryden House, Northampton, NN4 7DE.* Can offer advice on tree and landscape matters. Contact 01604 236236.

The Wildlife Trust for Northamptonshire. The main organisation which is working to conserve and enhance the wildlife environment in the county. In conjunction with Northampton Borough Council it manages reserves like Lings Wood, Barnes Meadow and Kingsthorpe Local Nature Reserve within the Borough Boundary. In addition it is consulted on a range of topics by various groups and organisations, including Northampton Borough Council. Apart from joining the organisation it is possible to get involved with conservation work. For more details contact the Wildlife Trust for Northamptonshire at Lings House, Billing Lings, Northampton, NN3 4BE. 01604 405285.

INDEX

A

Abington Park 9, 12
Africa 27
Ants 38, 69
Aphids 88
Ash 24

B

Badby 40
Badger 17, 38, 76, 81
Barnes Meadow 46, 50
Basket Maker 43
Bats 82
Beech 11
Bees 38, 63, 69, 70, 76, 78, 80, 87, 88
Birds 78-80
Blackbird 10, 24, 28, 31, 36, 52
Blackcap 24
Blackfly 88
Blue Fleabane 19
Borough Council 17, 72
Bradlaugh, Fields 13
Charles 13
Bracken 35, 38
Brambles 35
Bridge Street, 44
Bristletails 67
Brampton, Arm 30
Brook 40
Broomrape 15
BTCV 17
Buckler Fern 35
Buddle, Adam 51
Buddleia 44, 51, 80
Bumble Bee 15
Buttercups 30
Butterflies 30, 35, 42, 46, 48, 51, 66, 70, 74, 76, 78. 80, 82, 90, 91

C

Canada Geese 12, 26
Carp 48
Celandine 11
Centipede 70, 88, 89
Chaffinches 22, 28, 36
Chickweed 65
Chile Pine 11, 28
Chrysanthemum 19
Chub 32
Churches 57, 58
Compost 83, 84
Coot 12, 27
Coppice 35
Corn Bunting 18
Corn Marigold 19
Corn Spurrey 19
Cornflower 18
Cowslip 46
Cow Meadow 46
Cranesbill, dusky 12
pencilled 12
Crows 36
Cuckoo 26, 42
Curlew 41

D

Daffodils 21
Daisy 30
Dallington Fields 18
Damselfly 39, 42, 46, 48, 49
Dandelion 57, 65
Deadnettles 14
Delapre 20
Douglas Fir 35
Doves 52, 53
Dragonfly 39, 43, 46, 48, 49
Ducks 11
Dunnock 24
Duston 40, 42

E

Earwig 70
Eastfield Park 24
Elder Bush 52

F

Fern 15, 16, 61, 62
Field Mouse Ear 16
Figwort 44
Fireweed 52
Flowering Rush 47
Fox 38, 77, 81

G

Geraniums 12
Ginkgo 11
Golden Plover 47
Goldfinches 22
Goldings 19
Goose 34, 35
Grebe 22
Greenfinches 22, 28
Greenfly 88
Gulls 50, 54

H

Hawkweeds 58, 65
Harebells 16, 17
Haresfoot Clover 19
Harpole 35
Harts Tongue 21
Hazel 21, 36
Heather 34, 35
Hedgehog 76, 77, 81, 82
Hedges 72, 73, 74
Herons 50
Hills and Holes 13, 16
Holly 10, 20
Holton Lane 16
Horton 40
Hoverfly 37
Hydrangeas 20

I

Indian Balsam 45
Insects 80
Iris 25, 44
Ivy 63-67

J

Japanese Knotweed 44
John Lindley 10

K

Kingfisher 23
Kingsthorpe 30, 32, 35, 62, 63
Kislingbury 41
Knapweed 14

L

Lacewings 88
Ladybirds 88
Ladys Bedstraw 31, 32
Lady's Smock 42
Larch 35
Lichens 58-61, 66
Limestone 11, 16
Lings Wood 34-36, 38, 39, 57

M

Magnolias 20
Magpie 36
Mammals 80-82, 85
Manfield 24
Maidenhair Tree 11
Mallard 11, 26
Manor House 11
Maple 24
Marigold 31
Meadow Saxifrage 16, 21, 31
Mill, Duston 40-43

Upton 40
Weston Favell 46
Millipede 70, 88-90
Monkey Puzzle 11, 28
Moorhen 11, 12, 27
Mosses 58-61
Moths 90, 91
Mulberry 10
Muntjac 38, 77

N

Naseby 40
Nene Valley 27
Nene Washland 46, 50
Nettles 62, 65, 82
Northampton,
Abington Pk 56
All Saints 51, 55
Barnes Meadow 46, 50
Carlsberg 54
Castle 58, 75
Cloisters 75
Corporation 28
Doddridge Ch 62
Drapery 51, 55
Gasworks 44
Jeyes Jetty 55
Market Sq 53
Mayor 21
Midsummer M 46
Railway Station 44, 58
St Giles 55
St Katherines St 55
South Bridge 44
Town Centre 51, 55
Water Ski Club 22
West Bridge 44, 62
Northamptonshire,
Red Data Book 13
Norway Spruce 35

O

Obelisk 35
Overstone 35
Orchid 15,
Bee 15
Spotted 15
Owl, short-eared 41

P

Parsley, Corn 14
Cow 13
Pheasants 34
Pigeon 36, 52, 53
Pike 22
Pocket Parks 72-75
Blackthorn 72
Boughton Lane 73
Great Billing 74
Levi Strauss 74
Nettle Gap 74, 75
Officer 75
Spring Bor's 74, 75
Wootton 75
Podsol 35
Ponds 83
Pondweed 23
Punch Tree 10

Q

Quail 18

R

Rabbits 38
Ramshorns 23, 32, 41
Ragged Robin 31
Redshank 32, 40
Redstart 53
Redwing 31
Reed 25, 26
Reed Bunting 45
Reed Warbler 26
Restharrow 15
Rhododendron 35, 36
Ridge and Furrow 22
River Nene 30, 40-50
Roach 32
Robin 53, 55, 70
Rosebay willowherb 51, 52

S

Sallow 44
Scots Pine 35
Scrub Field 13, 16, 17
Sedge 25, 42
Sedge Warbler 26
Silver Birch 35
Silverfish 66, 67
Sixfields 40, 42
Skylarks 32
Snails 32, 41, 67
Snipe 32
South Bridge 44
Sparrow 52, 53, 55, 66
Sparrow Hawk 32
Spiders 67-69, 86, 87
Spleenwort 62
Spring Lane Sch 75
Springtails 66
Squirrel 28, 38, 55
Staverton 40
Starlings 37, 50, 52-55
Stickleback 33
Stinkhorn 36
Stonechat 49, 50
Stonecrop 45, 58, 63, 64
Stone Habitats 82, 85, 86
Stormcock 29
Stortons Pit 43
Swans 40
Sycamore 36
Sywell, 35
Country Pk 27

T

Tern 27
Thistles 49, 65
Thornton 28
Thrushes 10, 24, 28, 37, 38, 52
Tulip Tree 20

U

Upton 40

V

Vetch 25
Vole, Water 32

W

Wagtail 32, 54
Wallflower 57, 65
Walls 56-71
Wasps 65, 66, 69, 70
Waterlily 32, 41, 44
Wellingtonia 10, 20
Westone 34
White Poplar 30
Whitwood 21
Wildlife Garden 76-91
Wildlife Trust 13, 16, 17, 34, 46
Willow 43, 44
Willow Herbs 36
Willow Warbler 36
Witches Eggs 37
Woodlice 67, 85
Woodpecker 24, 37
Wootton Brook 40
Wren 70, 71